T0095525

# SPIRITUAL LESSONS FOR 21ˢᵀ CENTURY CHURCH LEADERS

*"I had toiled; and indeed all was vanity and grasping for the wind. There was no profit under the sun"*
*(Ecclesiastes 2:11 NKJV).*

**Meric D. Walker,**
**Trevor O'Reggio**

authorHOUSE®

*AuthorHouse™*
*1663 Liberty Drive*
*Bloomington, IN 47403*
*www.authorhouse.com*
*Phone: 1-800-839-8640*

*Cover design by Jim Patterson*
*Typeset: 12pt. New Times Romans by M. D. walker*
*Contact address: mericwalker@yahoo.com*

*Published by AuthorHouse    07/11/2012*

*ISBN: 978-1-4772-1991-1 (sc)*
*ISBN: 978-1-4772-1990-4 (e)*

*Library of Congress Control Number: 2012910505*

# DEDICATED

to all the wonderful Christian leaders throughout all
Christian organizations

# ACKNOWLEDGMENT

We are indebted to the many church leaders whom we have observed over the past thirty years. They unknowingly, by their church governance have provided important data for this project. We particularly admire and are appreciative of a few retired church leaders who, through their private chamber's reflection, voluntarily gave indispensable lessons from their own mistakes in church administration.

The realization of this project, *Church Politics: Spiritual Lessons For 21st Century Church Leaders*, was certainly not our sole effort, but inclusively the product of those who stood by us intellectually and practically, because for them also, proper governance of God's church is most vital. However, we are most grateful to God who has chosen to use us as a medium through which He Himself has produced *Church Politics: Spiritual Lessons For 21st Century Church Leaders*. We believe this book will be a helpful resource toward spiritual church administration by converted church leaders worldwide.

# TABLE OF CONTENTS

# PREFACE

This book can change your life in many ways. It provides information about the behavioral practices in the governance of many church organizations and the spiritual implications of these practices. While it is about information, it is more about spiritual transformation. It is about building a personal relationship with Christ and constantly beholding him as your Model Leader.

This account is "layreader friendly" and useful to pastors, seminary students, administrators in all sectors of church operation, and perhaps helpful to all workers in the cause of Christ.

The overall breadth of the chapters covers a spectrum of issues relating to church governance. The need for and the scope of the book are pinned down in the first chapter; each of the other chapters is divided into two sections: (1) descriptive behavioral trends observed in church governance within many church organizations, and (2) prescriptive Bible-based spiritual lessons.

There is a widespread feeling that Christlikeness is greatly lacking in the governance of many churches. Behaviors pertaining to lack of trust in God to guide one's future; convenient passion for Christ linked to leadership position; faked spirituality; misuse of preaching; silence regarding sin; wrong motive pertaining to praise, promotion, and punishment; inconsistence in the use of policy, procedure, and protocol; inappropriate disclosure of private information; friendship without brotherhood; discipleship without spiritual disciplines; the wrong use of church resources; self-centered legacy; fear as a political tactic; humor toward self-benefit; grief abuse and misuse toward a selfish end; use of education as a liability; selfish actions toward undoing, redoing, and outdoing predecessor's achievements; and the outworking of an unconverted conscience, are all factors highlighted which negatively impact church governance.

Keeping in mind that each church has its strengths and challenges, come with us on this spiritual trek. Fear not! Be open-minded as we critically look together at church politics within the church itself and its spiritual implications. Ask God for spiritual maturity and insights, not only for yourself, but for all members of the Christian faith, and pledge based on the formation of His character in you, to do your part in rightly representing Him in church operations.

# IN BEGINNING

*"That you may be filled with the knowledge*
*of His will in all wisdom and*
*spiritual understanding"*
(Colossians 1: 9 NKJV).

In as much as several volumes have been written, numerous articles penned, and persuasive speeches delivered on the issue of whether or not Christians have a role in state-politics, there remains a greater need for the chronicling of critical thoughts regarding politics within the church itself. It is spiritually important to examine the church itself in relation to its own internal operations.

In the context of the Great Controversy between Christ and Satan, and the Great Commission to go and make disciples of Christ, the intent of this book is to unearth indispensable spiritual lessons for 21$^{st}$ century church leaders.

## Definitions

Although church is generally defined as a collection of Christian organizations, which is inspired by, and seeks to represent, the significance of Jesus' ministry, it also pertains to a single church "denomination."

The word politics is believed to be derived from the backdrop of early formation of popular rule in ancient democratic governance which replaced tyrannies in the early 5th century BC in many Greek cities.[1]

For our discussion on church politics and spirituality let us be guided by Plunkitt's dictum that the stuff of good politics constitutes respect for human needs, values, and beliefs.[2]

Church politics is the organized conduct of relationships associated with the administration and governance of the church, based on the mindset, views, and pursuits of church people, especially church leaders. Are there biblical guidelines for church politics? Is it always sacred and good, or is it innately evil and something to be tabooed by the Christian religion? Are the "saints" always sober and sanctified in their administration and governance of God's work?

In God's work, good politics is Christ-centered and mission-oriented, consistent in godly wisdom, without malice, exhibiting respect and dignity, and embracing the worth of each member of the body of

Christ. This is necessary in the operations of any truly Christian organization.

Organized conduct of relationships that is of Christian dignity and Christlike purity, guided by the golden rule in concert with the question "What would Jesus have me do?" is unequivocally descriptive of good church politics.

On the other hand, whenever activities associated with the administration and governance of the church are intentionally carried out mainly to improve or maintain the organizational status or rank of individuals toward self-benefits, then such politics, based on the mission Christ gave to His church, is definitely bad church politics.

Bad church politics is individually-centered and through the foolishness of human "wisdom," more often than not, whether covertly or overtly, exhibits unethical, ungodly, immoral, or even inhumane demeanor that at times wounds deeply, leaving spiritual, psychological, financial, or social transgenerational scars. This is detestable in any truly Christian organization.

Although good church politics is seemingly inevitable in the proper operations of any faith community, the general preponderance of bad conducts in church operations causes the term "church politics" to derive a negative meaning in the minds of most members of many church organizations.

Consequently, recently, the chief church leader for an entire region, in what is now known as his exit speech, spoke passionately of "church politics" being negative in general, saying that he studied it, he practiced it, but now church leaders must put it away and grow up to maturity. Because such church leader did not stay in church leadership after this speech, no one will ever know whether or not he was converted to doing better. Hence, the sincerity of his speech is questioned.

This book focuses on such derived general view that "church politics" is bad and counter to the proper operations of God's church. Therefore, it highlights bad church politics and points out spiritual lessons toward good church governance. In whatever context, the heeding of these recommendations no doubt will result in church operations that are Christ-centered.

## The Sour Grape Syndrome

A popular animal animated story: A fox in desperation to satisfy its hunger, repeatedly stretched itself, leaped as high as it could, and climbed as skillfully as naturally gifted, in an effort to reach some apparently succulent grapes.

With depleted energy, failure, and disappointment, its hunger was not abated because it could not reach the grapes. Consequently, the fox was not satisfied until it mentally pampered itself concluding that the grapes were not worth the effort because, though untasted, they were "sour."

In the operations of the church, many church people find themselves in the company of the fox. Having not gotten their desired church leadership positions, they mentally satisfy themselves that to hold a church position is systemically "bad," and consequently all those who hold such positions, practiced "church politics" to get there and played it to stay there. Beware of this sour grape syndrome! Caution against the sweeping generalization that all church leaders do dirty politics, is taken within this book.

While it is true that not all church leaders are committed servants of God, and that many are in their leadership positions because of unprincipled acts of church politics, one must be careful in classifying the operations of the church as bad or evil. Church operations are not bad or good based on whether or not such meet one's personal, family members,' or friends' expectations. Classifications and conclusions regarding the church' operations must be based on moral and ethical Christ-centered principles.

The biblical framework of church operations anchors that God works through many earthly elected or selected church leaders. The more He is allowed to dwell in them, the more their operations reflect Him. It is good to be a good church leader.

**Index to Character**
In every context, the activities and attitudes displayed in church politics fall into the A-Z components

of the character of church people, chief of whom are leaders.

Jesus Himself declares: "Therefore by their fruits you will know them" (Matthew 7: 20, NKJV). And the fruit of the Spirit that must be demonstrated by members to one another and to others, as they carry out activities associated with the governance of the church, is "Love, joy, peace, longsuffering, kindness, goodness, faithfulness, gentleness, self-control" (Galatians 5: 22, 23, NKJV).

These foregoing characteristics are surely seen to be present or absent in the concepts and conducts of church members, chief of whom are leaders as they guide the ongoing activities of the church, and also as they periodically exercise their ecclesiastical political franchise in choosing individuals to lead out in particular ministries at all levels in God's work.

## A Special Privilege

Just to be a Christian is a spiritual privilege, because despite Adam's failure, based on grace, God affords each of us a second chance to know Him personally and to be with Him eternally.

The purpose of the church as a faith community is to help each person to fully utilize this privilege of salvation. To be a leader in the church, whether in a local congregation or at other organizational levels, carries with it the most sacred responsibility of enhancing and helping individuals grow in Christ.

Is not it a very fearful thing to be a church leader at any level? It ought to be. The responsibility to do the Lord's biddings is an awesome one. Church leadership is certainly not for persons who desire to be lorded as it were they are divine sparks or extensions of God Himself.

Leadership is not for those who long and thirst for position in order to feel special and progressive. It is not for the proud and self-centered. It is not for those who merely pretend to know God. Is it not for servants who are being spiritually formed into the fullness of God's ideal?

Whether a member serves as an officer in the local church, or as pastor, teacher, principal, president, director, dean, secretary, or computer programmer etc, once the job description enhances the mission of the church, it is definitely a special privilege within limited time.

This privilege of leading must be spiritually executed with the critical ingredients of godly fear and Christlike humility.

# SPIRITUAL LESSONS FROM
# TWO MODELS

*"Now listen! Today I am giving you a choice between
life and death, between prosperity and disaster"*
(Deuteronomy 30: 15-16 NLT).

Although the word politics is not found in the Bible, it proliferates through the pages of Holy Writ and anchors, through multiple incidents, essential spiritual guidelines for the operation of God's church, not just for Bible times and other times, but for this time.

## Condescension versus Exaltation

Leadership models derived from the context of the beginning of the Great Controversy between Christ and Satan in heaven, set before 21st century church leaders two models: one that is other-centered, and the other, self-centered; one that is focused on spiritually enriching the lives of others while the other is based on self-benefit.

Lucifer, an angel created by God, although already exalted as "shining one" not only desired to be further exalted, but also to get the office that rightly belongs to God. He no doubt believed that in that office he would get sacred worship, more respect, more honor, more dominion, access to more resources, more authority, and more freedom. In seeking to get, "he was corrupted" and therefore became "fallen" (Isaiah 14: 12-14; and Ezekiel 28: 17) as Satan the prince of demons (Matthew 3: 22).

Would the sad reality of not truly accepting God as head and the pride to exalt self end there? Or, would it infect, affect, and inflict people far into the 21st century? Is God's church susceptible to Lucifer's sin of self-exaltation? This sin of Lucifer was the beginning of the politics of ascent.

The politics of descent on the other hand, when the earth was lost by Adam to Satan, was modeled by Jesus:

*"Being in very nature God,*
*did not consider equality with God*
*Something to be used to his own advantage;*
*rather, he made himself nothing*
*by taking the very nature of a servant,*
*being made in human likeness.*
*And being found in appearance as a man,*
*he humbled himself*

*by becoming obedient to death—*
*even death on a cross!"*
(Philippians 2: 5-8 NIV).

## Servant versus Superior

The preceding text describes the descent of Jesus as taking on the form of a servant. The Greek word for servant here is *doulos* and is stronger than our English word for servant. It means slave. Jesus' decent to the earth was not just as human but the lowest kind of human—a slave. He could have come with royal pedigree, or aristocratic lineage, or middle class stock, but he chose to come as the lowest of the low. What does that mean for church leaders who aspire to follow His example of servant leadership?

The servant leader serves first and then leads after. This is very different from those leaders who aspire for leadership positions then choose to serve out of moral or obligatory reasons. Servant leaders are not seeking or aspiring after leadership positions, but simply want to serve, so that leadership flows from their desire to serve. Their goal or mission is not to lead but to serve. Leadership is always secondary, so that if they are removed from leadership positions, they are not mad or angry because a leadership position was never their aim. On the contrary, their desire to serve remains unabated. In Mark 9:35, Jesus says, if any one wants to be first, he shall be last of all and servant of all.

One writer describes a number of characteristics of a servant leader:

1. The leader guides
2. The leader is goal oriented and qualified
3. The leader listens and reflects
4. The leader is fair and flexible
5. The leader is aware and intuitive
6. The leader uses persuasion
7. The leader takes one step at a time.[1]

How are people affected by this kind of servant leadership? People associated with servant leadership become healthier, wiser, freer, and more autonomous. In addition, the least privileged of society are helped and are not further deprived. This positive impact upon those whom the servant leader leads, arises out of the desire to serve others rather than to magnify self. Servant leaders will spend time with their followers, understand their needs and abilities, ask their opinions, seek their input and provide resources necessary for them to be successful in their roles.

The leadership model of Jesus is primarily that of a servant. The main leadership mistake of church leaders is the top-down, bossy, autocratic, military model of being superior to underlings and being fully in charge. [2]

## Divine Model versus Human Model

In the *Divine Model*, God's example, counsel, and authority are the ultimate points of reference for church operation. Being the absolute embodiment of knowledge and wisdom, He Himself is the Divine Model for church administrators.

**Unity and Love.** In unity and oneness of purpose, the members of the Godhead, Father, Son, and Holy Spirit, do not contrive against, compare with, and compete in opposition to one another, but divinely consolidate, cooperate and commune regarding humanity's salvation, the purpose for which the Christian church has always existed.

**Attitude and Behavior.** In Christ's earthly life, His attitude of humility, respect and love for all persons, provide examples of how leadership positions, giftedness, and natural competencies must be used to affirm and help people to better their lives on earth and more importantly to prepare for more than the temporal material world, but for eternal abundant life.

*Human Model* in relation to church operations is an extreme misrepresentation of the model of God's governance. It is a somewhat sacrilegious comedy lacking spiritual seriousness and soberness. As such its decisions and actions are counterproductive to personal spiritual growth and the advance of God's Kingdom of Grace.

**Self-centeredness.** The human model of church governance is a first person singular obsession and passion for earthly status that satisfies the "ego." It is untouched by purposeful godly love, and is blinded by position, tainted by pride, and suckled by self-centeredness.

The Divine Model counsels: "Look unto me . . . all the ends of the earth: for I am God, and there is none else" (Isaiah 45: 22, KJV). W. D. Longstaff's timely admonition is instructive:

> *"Take time to be holy,*
> *be calm in thy soul. Thus led by His Spirit,*
> *to fountains of love, thou soon shall be fitted for*
> *service above."*[3]

## Maturity versus Immaturity

The spiritual maturity of church leaders is indispensable for proper church governance.

Spiritual maturity is a construct of religious growth in which a person develops through continuous critical self-reflection not relying on the support of others to maintain religious beliefs and practice.[4] Spiritually mature Christians are those who have through continuous critical reflection grown in their relationship with God to the extent where they maintain closeness and communion with Him irrespective of the beliefs and practice of others.[5]

Through such continual encounter God inspires, illuminates, and motivates true Christian leaders, making them perceptive, knowledgeable, and wise in their execution of power.

Spiritually immature church leaders lack such closeness and communion with God. This causes them to misrepresent Him in the concepts and behaviors they exercise in their governance of the church.

However, such misrepresentation by immature church leaders should not make spiritually mature Christians lose faith in God, or make them bitter with one another. Despite the weaknesses of any church leader, mature Christians will not cherish retaliation, stifling the mission or slowing the march of God's church.

Mature Christians always want to do much toward advancing God's work. Such attitude is an essential fruit of true Christian conversion—the born again experience.

## Conclusive Spiritual Lessons

Spiritual leaders must take their cue from observing how God, from time immemorial, has meticulously guided His people. The characteristics of God are demonstrated in what He does. While church leaders are not able to be like God pertaining to His sovereignty and power, in the human sphere they can be like Him in quality pertaining to indispensable virtues for church governance and in living the Christian life in general. The apostle Paul declares, "I can do all things through

Christ who strengthens me" (Philippians. 4: 13 NKJV). He further instructs: "Imitate me, just as I also imitate Christ" (1 Corinthians. 11: 1 NKJV).

## Anchor Points

Condescension, humility, servant leadership, unity toward salvation, and genuine spirituality, are all modeled by God in the Bible as indispensable elements for church governance. Accordingly Jeremiah 9: 23-24 (NKJV) admonish:

*"Let not the wise man glory in his wisdom.*
*Let not the mighty man glory in his might,*
*Nor let the rich man glory in his riches; But*
*Let him who glories glory in this, that he*
*understands and knows me."*

# SPIRITUAL LESSONS FROM CHURCH
# POLITICS PERTAINING TO
# THE UNKNOWN

*"He changes the times and the seasons; He removes
kings and raises up kings"*
(Daniel 2: 21 NKJV).

In what ways is the unknown a causative factor for politicking in some church organizations? How does a hierarchical church culture contribute to church politics?

## The Known

Many church members, some of whom are employed to carry out the mission of the church, are side-tracked by setting their gaze on, and wanting to be the persons holding particular church leadership positions or offices. For many of these individuals, holding leadership positions is an indicator of progress at its best on that particular denominational landscape.

**Hierarchical Hurdle**. By and large, the belief that true progress is moving up in the church hierarchy is nurtured by the practices of many church organizations. These church organizations practice a too pronounced, distinct, and discriminatory hierarchical model of remuneration and personal benefits to workers. This becomes even more blatant in the face of great remuneration disparity based on hierarchy of workers, notwithstanding similar years of service and qualification.

Some undesirable demarcations and exclusions based on leadership-levels are cited by some church members who were asked whether or not they are concerned about demarcations and exclusions based on hierarchy in their own church organization:

1. In many instances at church functions, church leaders are catered for differently in setting and contents based on their grouped leadership levels. For example, one person noted that for meals at church functions leaders at "high levels" sit and are served adequately with the best cutlery while other leaders at "low levels" join long frustrating lines to collect their meager meals in boxes.

2. Leaders are given special untenable allowances and emoluments that are not available to other workers.

3. Leaders' relatives and friends are often guaranteed work by the leaders themselves and are strategically placed within and across the organization's grid, while other persons, though qualified for available jobs, are often last and least considered.

5. Leaders' photographs are generally conspicuously mounted on walls in hallways and general areas of churches' headquarters depicting ranks and reign while many productive and committed workers' photographs never have a place on any wall within the buildings of their organization.

6. The offices occupied by top church leaders are in some cases constructed with superiorly different tiles, doors, windows, lighting fixtures, are more spacious, and are equipped with the best furniture, and have the best amenities compared to the offices of church leaders on lower levels.

Though young and seemingly more educated, many leaders have not climbed out of the bad traditions of some of their predecessors. By their own attitudes and behaviors, the leaders themselves, subtly rivet in the minds of those whom they lead, that higher level leaders are "brighter, better, and richer" when compared with leaders on lower levels.

This *known* is further compounded in cases where the magnitude of retirement benefits is determined based on the so-called highest position the retiree served in his or her active years. In some church organizations, persons who are leaving the organization or an institution, by transfer, retirement, or resignation, receive gifts, whether given in private or in public, generally reflecting rank in value.

Based on discriminatory hierarchism of benefits created by many church organizations, many if not most church workers want to be the leaders of highest ranks. The sense of being at an advantage or disadvantage based on whether or not one holds a high leadership office, dominates the minds of many church employees. Whenever the forgoing factors exist within any church organization, it makes the church increasingly polarized.

Many denominational employees are caught in the web of seeing those holding leadership positions as being better than those who do not. Consequently, when such leadership positions or offices are not quickly forthcoming for these persons, they become very disappointed, discouraged, and disheartened, believing that they are a failure in their chosen profession.

To a great extent, new workers are brain-washed and socially influenced with this church culture, and the vicious cycle continues, and paradoxically in certain cases and many places, worsens as the work of the church geographically and numerically expands.

## The Unknown

Generally many employees seem to despise the "unknown" about their future. They are challenged by it. They want to know. They want to make certain it goes their way. They want to do something about it. For them, today's acts are not really for today's benefits, but they are for tomorrow's security. They worry about tomorrow. Paradoxically, making the best of today is often cancelled by an obsession with tomorrow. Consequently, they really do not live in the "now," they reside in the "future."

**Human as God**. Napoleon Hill's hallmark expression of success that "what the mind of man can conceive and believe, it can achieve"[1] is deeply entrenched in the philosophy of church people. Unequivocally, this theory has its benefits in helping people to dream big and positively pursue the dream. However, whenever this belief is applied to church positions, in the context of a hierarchical structure, it tends to affect individual spirituality and infect the church's operations.

Although God equips each church worker with gifts-talents, it is never meant to place church leaders in God's stead or as His head. Is not God prudent enough, powerful enough, and present enough to reign as the Head of His church?

**The Craftiest.** The future is unknown to humankind but known to God. Without faith in God who knows and directs the unknown, humankind is vulnerable to try and carve out a future that is not in conformity to God's will. On the one hand, many church members because they do not trust God with their future in relation to their holding or not holding particular so-called prestigious and benefit-gaining positions in church work, wrongly get involved in planning, canvassing, and scheming for such positions. More often than not such canvassing or vote solicitation results in the belittling of others, the attempting to deform character, the severing of friendship, the polarizing of membership, and the stymieing of church mission.

The obvious premise for these actions is that of human effort not merely to make an unknown future known, but to create it toward personal benefit. Given time, these behaviors and actions are replicated and quickly become ingrained in the church culture, and therefore, political craftiness becomes so-called dependable prophetic means to determine and unveil the unknown on behalf of the craftiest.

**No Canvassing, Please.** In some cases there is spiritual abuse in which the incumbents because they have the power, the pulpit, and denominational respect to exhort, to instruct, to demand and command those over whom they rule, they instruct them not to be involved in the solicitation of votes because it is "unspiritual and wrong" to do so. Consequently, out of the reservoirs of their Christian virtues many members obey by not getting involved in the solicitation of votes for their preferred leaders. They cool out and prayerfully wait for the election outcome.

However, to their amazement, the same incumbent leaders smile and sometimes laugh subtly and get their well organized political machinery rolling, and sometimes this machinery is better organized than that of state politics. This is a form of spiritual abuse.

**Hijacked**. In some church culture the main church leader is seen as the superior to all other leaders. In such culture, the other levels of leaders usually support the decisions and directions of the main leader. To do otherwise is to be seen as uncooperative. That leader knows he or she is superior in that sense. Hence, the expression "the President's church" aptly applies to some church organizations to the extent that he or she has full way and sway pertaining to decisions whether these be good or bad for the church at large.

Because church organizations generally operate on a constitution that allows church leaders to be chosen by a democratic process involving church members other than the incumbent church leaders themselves, at that time the church members as a group are technically superior to any church leader. See Figure 1.

But as mentioned earlier, quite often the electoral process is hijacked through politicking. While verbally praying for the Lord to lead, leaders predetermine who must really lead and thereby set up political schemes to effect their decisions through nominating committees.

In such cases, the church leaders go full circle as superiors technically and practically abusing the people's theoretical superiority.

**Bigger Plan**. In a desperate effort to hold on to their positions, many incumbent church leaders seek to jeopardize the electing of persons who have talents and competencies for leadership, by politically smudging, ostracizing criticizing, dismissing, and reassigning them.

Leaders who practice such behaviors obviously in their minds believe that they have reached their height of their power, or the possibility of their moving upwardly is dependent on holding on to their present positions for some more time. They cannot see God leading them into His 'choicest' service, even if it is not their desired leadership position. Therefore, they fight to keep their position of Head Master, Director, Manager, President etc, while God is somewhat hindered to unfold His "bigger" plans for them.

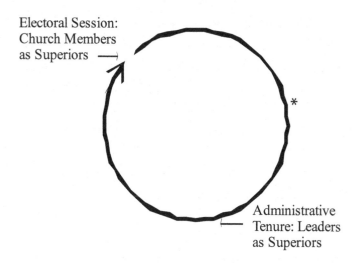

Electoral Session:
Church Members
as Superiors  ⟶

Administrative
Tenure: Leaders
as Superiors

*Figure 1.* The circle of church governance illustrating the long administrative tenure in which church leaders have superiority as compared to a short period of superiority held by church people who elect those leaders at electoral sessions.

\* Administrative tenure of leadership of one main leader whom other church leaders follow subserviently is **usually not smooth** emotionally.

### Conclusive Spiritual Lessons

The problems of the "unknown" pertaining to church politics with reference to seeking leadership positions, span concepts, attitudes, and behaviors regarding success, and trust in God

**Definition of Success**. Critical thinking about success, encompasses analysis of the dimensions of life, namely, the physical, social, mental, and spiritual.

Each of these is categorized as either being temporal or eternal. For the Christian, the overarching dominant one, as the fundamental reference point for the others. It is the spiritual which has eternal consequences. Consequently, spirituality filters all the others in beliefs, attitudes and behaviors appropriate for eternity.

Success for the Christian is not merely progressing against mitigating forces and circumstances, to reach a state defined by society as "good or great," but it is pressing to a spiritual standing that takes precedence in the line of physical, social, and mental achievements.

One Bible Instructor used to say "Hitch your wagon to a star." He meant seek to achieve even the seemingly impossible in the temporal sphere of earthly achievements but at all times be spiritually attached to Christ the Morning Star.

True ultimate success is to be healthy, happy, safe, and most of all being in a conscious, learning, discovering loving relationship with God and His people for eternity. That is worth dying for.

No person must allow actual or perceived hierarchical discriminatory disparities to relegate and confine his or her concept of success to earthly benefits derived from being in leadership positions. In some cases, the higher the positions, the more bitter the persons. Heaven is to be the top-ranked goal:

> *"But seek first the kingdom of God and*
> *His righteousness"*
> (Matthew 6: 33 ESV).

> *"My food is to do the will of Him who sent me,*
> *and to finish His work"*
> (John 4: 34 ESV).

> *"I press toward the goal for the prize of the upward*
> *call of God in Christ Jesus"*
> (Philippians 3: 14 ESV).

**True Greatness**. True greatness is found in Christlike humility. However, the concept of being more progressive than one's colleague, merely because of a leadership position, does not reflect true greatness. This has nothing to do with Christlike impact on people's lives, but, more often than not, is about popularity, remuneration, personal benefits, and the promotion of "ego."

**Trust in God**. Trust in God is an essential characteristic of being Christian. Lack of it indicates a serious spiritual problem. *Trust* in God is unwavering acceptance of God as the supreme omnipotent Head of the church. Each member ought to faithfully depend on Him to superbly guide and manage all challenges of life.

Christians are quick to say "Trust in the Lord," but in many instances many Christian church workers are quick to put the Lord aside and seek to carve out their own destiny in relation to their quest for high church office. The Bible advises: "Trust in the Lord with all thine heart; and lean not unto thine own understanding. In all thy ways acknowledge him, and he shall direct thy paths" (Proverbs 3: 5-6 KJV).

Allowing Him to direct "your paths" requires waiting. Of such the psalmist proclaims: "Wait on the Lord: be of good courage, and he shall strengthen thine heart: wait, I say, on the Lord" (Psalm 27: 14 KJV).

*Examples of Bible characters*. Abraham's faith in God propelled him into the unknown. His obsession was not earthly but his mind was occupied with the heavenly and it caused him to strive for a city whose builder and maker was God. Consequently, he pleased God in being willing to slay his only son. God Himself promoted him as the father-leader of all nations

Joseph's brothers consulted, conspired, and connived against him in an effort to determine what their future would not be. They sold him into the unknown. He clung tenaciously to principles of right thinking and living and waited on the Lord. He was elevated by the Lord to becoming the second most powerful man throughout Egypt and leader over his same conniving brothers.

Moses, after standing up and putting his life on the line for his fellow man who was being brutally beaten, was banished to die in the unknown by Pharaoh. But he was elevated by God as one of the most powerful leaders of all times. More than that though, he was resurrected and taken to heaven.

Daniel was taken captive by the Babylonian army into the unknown. He was faithful to God in his lifestyle including diet, commitment to the right, and the discipline of prayer. God promoted him to high leadership position against the odds of being likely to be chosen for that position being a foreign captive.

Not being willing to wait on the Lord and trusting His leading for one's future, is an indication of a serious spiritual.

### Anchor Points

Christians must place their spirituality and relationship with Christ as their priority in life. They must in all cases in all things genuinely seek to reflect the mind and lifestyle of Christ.

To desire leadership positions in church work is not of itself wrong. But caution must be taken that it is desired for righteous reasons.

Character matters most. Surrounding one's self with positive, genuine, influential persons is wise but friendship that is merely based on expected leadership-position-derived personal benefit is wrong.

Supporting a person as your choice for a church leadership position is certainly natural. Such support must be based on genuine assessment of the person being the most suitable for the execution of the job description. Concepts, attitudes, and behaviors at all times to all persons in all places must be Christlike.

Do not be caught up with opposing persons for leadership positions, be more concerned about supporting persons whom you believe are competent and spiritual to do the Master's biddings.

Any action that seeks to suppress and punish people because of their personal choice of leaders is not only a violation of those persons' human rights, but it is a signal of disrespect for the wisdom of God who gave humankind the freedom of choice.

If you are pushing yourself for a leadership position, it just does not seem right and spiritual. Be willing to admit your mistakes. Change!

As God's royal people, leave the unknown to Him, wait patiently, live holy, and you will see the ultimate unfolding of His plan for you from now to eternity. "Therefore, humble yourselves under the mighty hand of God, so that at the proper time he may exalt you" (1 Peter 5: 6 ISV).

# SPIRITUAL LESSONS FROM CHURCH POLITICS PERTAINING TO PASSION

*"They have a zeal for God but not according to
knowledge. For they being ignorant of
God's righteousness, and seeking to
establish their own righteousness,
have not submitted to
the righteousness
of God"*

(Romans 10: 2, 3 NKJV).

What is Christian passion? Is it a means to or a product of church leadership positions? Are church positions justifiable havens for the burnt-out and the passionless? Is passion an inevitable output of conversion? Can passion be faked?

## Christian Passion

Christian passion or indispensable zeal to carry out the mission of Christ is enthusiasm derived and sustained from a personal relationship with Christ as one's Savior and Master. It is identified by the Prophet Jeremiah and tuned in a Negro Spiritual as "Something within me like a burning fire." Passion brings every faculty into display, the heart bleeds, the body gestures, and the intellect is logically and substantially coherent.

**Part-time Half-hearted Service for Full-time Remuneration.** Many church workers have no passion and drive for the church's mission to which they have been called and employed. Their energy wanes, their drive retires, and their interest in the Lord's mission lukewarm. For the passionless pastor, there is no fire in the pulpit, no heart turning appeal for the rescue of souls, no thirst for godly deeds, no excitement of conversion, no push for visitation, and no enjoyment of accomplishment. In this case there is part-time half-hearted service for full-time remuneration.

## Political Passion

In some church organizations, whenever the time for the election of church leaders draws near, "like a rushing mighty wind" there is a surge of energy that erupts and a sudden seemingly insatiable burning interest for the mission of the church, demonstrated in the attitudes and behaviors of many church workers who desire to be chosen by being elected to available leadership positions.

In many cases, such convenient seasonal passion is the behavior of both the incumbents and others who desire to be the ones placed in particular leadership positions. Many workers have a passion to be the leader, and generally only a minuscule few have the drive to be good followers.

This becomes more complex and no doubt dangerous when such faked-passion is not short lived but is maintained over an extended period of time although not derived from a genuine walk with the Master. In some cases there is only apparent passion for the achievements that are expected and inspected by the organization, such as the amount of persons baptized, money collected, students enrolled, exams passed etc. Such organizational culture jeopardizes spirituality. What about passion for how people, God's crown of creation and objects of redemption are treated? What about excitement for the critical values that make people true Christians?

In many church organizations, many church workers who are lazy, cold, without a good track record of performance and work ethic, are destructively critical of the job description their organization stipulates for them complaining that it is not right and appropriate for the 21st century, but as soon as these same persons are elected or appointed by one means or another to leadership positions, they themselves from their new positions, instantly become paragons of organizational virtues, and passionately demand full compliance from those whom they now lead. Is such passion genuine? Many persons fake passion for political mileage of gaining and keeping leadership positions. Consequently, whenever these types of persons are not re-voted into leadership position, like a mirage their passion disappears.

**Lack of Passion Linked to Leadership Positions**. At the same time, politics of passion to a lesser extent also applies to using the office or leadership position as a refuge for the burnt-out, the passionless, and those who are failing. There are persons who campaign for leadership positions on the premise that "It is my time now. I am tired."

However, putting into leadership positions those who are tired and passionless regarding involvement in the mission of the church, results in stalling the advancing thrust of the Great Commission.

Leaders who are not passionate do not easily motivate people. Because of lack of interest, they will sometimes miss important appointments; make excuses; embarrass their organization and superiors; lack performance; lack vision; and tend to be easily pressured by challenges.

## Passion and Dynamism

Christian passion and dynamism go hand in hand. Passion is from the heart as described earlier, while dynamism is the high effervescence of energy and warmth with which a person serves, performs, and carries out through multiple means, the mission of Christ. Dynamism must be the genuine product of passion. Dynamism of church leaders can certainly be without passion. It can be mistaken for it by members who are undiscerning and those who have not had a reasonable time and suitable context to understand and analyze their leaders.

Many church leaders desiring to impress their people and superiors, intentionally design their speeches and reports with so-called passionate expressions and dynamic moods all skewed toward getting political support.

These leaders sometimes have a great fanfare preceding their delivery. They sometimes want the audio for themselves to be higher than those speakers who precede them. They use sighing tones when they are not really sighing; they use caring expressions without being caring; they use kind expressions without being kind; they use holy expressions without being holy; and loving expressions without being loving.

For example, if a school principal reports: "I love my teachers and give them regular salary increases," this principal really sounds loving and caring. But if it is known that each time the teacher gets an increase, the principal gets more increase than they do, and moreover the principal cannot get an increase without the teachers getting one too, the scenario of love certainly changes. In such cases passion is but pitfall.

## Passion and Physical Changes

Some church leaders desiring to impress their constituency that they are new and different seemingly become passionate about changes.

Sadly many of these church leaders focus only on changing the physical entities of their personal appearance, their office arrangement, their boardroom layout, their automobile, building colors, electronic gadgets and sometimes they even change their good friends. However, they keep their bad philosophies and practices regarding the operation of the work of God.

To be enthusiastic only about physical changes toward one's own credit and not passionate about Christian virtues is a bad bout of narcissism.

## Conclusive Spiritual Lessons

The politics of passion constitutes serious spiritual problems encompassing pretense for selfish gains, trivialization of sacred work, and definitely lack of conversion.

**Pretense.** Pretense is the deliberate conveyance or demonstration of a concept or behavior as one's value, although in reality it is not so.

Passion for God naturally flows from a heart that is overflowing with His love. Regarding God's people Titus notes: "His own special people, zealous for good works" (Titus 2:14 NKJV). When after the resurrection, on the Emmaus journey, Jesus disguised Himself and expounded the word concerning Himself to His disciples, and their respond was: "Did not our hearts burn within us?" (Luke 24: 32 NKJV).

Passion is a matter of the heart. It is not an event nor is it a program. It is a genuine response to the magnitude of the love of God. To fake it is presumption. Presumption is intricately linked to the sin against the Holy Spirit which is unpardonable. If our actions and words are not based on genuine love we are empty and meaningless. "Though I speak with the tongues of men and of angels, but have not love, I have become as sounding brass or a clanging cymbal" (1 Corinthians 13: 1 NKJV).

Pretense resulted in the death of Ananias and his wife Sapphira who pretended that they had fulfilled their pledge to give God all the proceeds from the sale of their property (See Acts 5: 1-11). Pretense led to the slaying of false prophets by Elijah. Pretense caused the possession of evil spirits. Pretense led to the rejection of the Jews as God people.

Passion must be for God and not for oneself. True passion is derived from an understanding and appreciation of the matchless love of God demonstrated in the redemptive history of salvation. Of such: "Behold what manner of love the Father has bestowed upon us, that we should be called the children of God! . . . we shall be like Him, for we shall see Him as He is" (1 John 3: 1, 2 NKJV).

**Trivialization of the Greatest Work on Earth.** In cases where church workers are placed in leadership positions for which they have no genuine passion, but merely because of friendship and personal gains, that is the trivialization of the great work of God.

God's work is serious business and to be a leader in His cause is the most serious and important work on earth. Such work is far greater than that of any position one holds in a community, state, nation, region, or on the world's arena. To fake being passionate about this great mission, is trivializing the work of God.

### Anchor Points

The essence of true passion is being in a state of saturation with the love of God to the extent that we overflow with true love for others and burn with enthusiasm to lead them to Christ.

Passion is not an act but it includes actions. It is not a position but it is powerful. It is not a reward but it is rewarding. True passion builds up right and seeks to tear down wrong. "But let him who glories glory in this, that he understands and knows me" (Jeremiah 9: 24 NKJV).

Whether persons are in a leadership position or not, Christians must have passion which mentally places them where others are at a disadvantage, and burns within them a sincere desire to lift those persons from their physical, spiritual, social, or metal disadvantage, to a higher plain. Genuine passion not only connects the Christians to Christ but intricately binds leaders to the led.

# SPIRITUAL LESSONS FROM CHURCH POLITICS PERTAINING TO RELIGIOSITY AND SPIRITUALITY

*"The natural man does not receive the things of the Spirit of God for they are foolishness to him; nor can he know them, because they are spiritually discerned"*

(1 Corinthians 2: 14 NKJV).

How is the difference between spirituality and religiosity played out in church politics? Is there a time to be spiritual and another time only to be religious?

## The Difference

*Spirituality* is the state of having God as one's ultimate reference for all beliefs and behaviors. To be guided by a power beyond human sphere lies at the heart of spirituality. *Religiosity* is the state of effecting religious rites such as attending church services, praying, fasting, studying the Bible, and sharing one's faith etc.

Spirituality ought to be the heart of religiosity. Spirituality has to do with right motives while religiosity has to do with right actions. Spirituality is internal while religiosity is external. Spirituality is known by God while religiosity is seen by humans. Spirituality is continual while religiosity is eventual. Spirituality is the root while religiosity is the branches. Spirituality is the spring from which religiosity flows. True religiosity is based on spirituality.

It is possible to have religious actions that are not spiritually based. Many persons just go through the motion of religious actions such as church attendance, prayer, fasting et etc, without having a deep relationship with God.

## Convenient Religiosity

Though visibly littered with people, building and other multiple resources, church organizations must be borne up by a spiritual foundation, without which, these organizations cannot accomplish their biblical mission.

**Pleasing the People**. Many church leaders focus mainly on the numerical growth of their church population and on financial increase of their organizations over time. In many cases while these areas of emphasis do very well, the church members themselves accuse their leaders of not being spiritual.

These leaders then become unpopular with the people. Having seen their leadership positions as being in jeopardy, they generally act quickly to save their positions. These leaders act merely "carrying out the motion" to please the people. In some cases, not only the incumbents, but those who are not in leadership position but desire to be, masquerade religiosity as spirituality before the people who demand it.

**Increasing Religiosity**. In the foregoing condition of criticism of being unspiritual, many church leaders rather than personally agonizing with the Lord for spiritual growth, merely increase events of religiosity and demand the attendance of the people.

More often than not there is no personal change in the lives of these leaders regarding morality, humility, and servanthood. At the same time, for them, religiosity becomes events to be had in full attendance, merely for the sake of reducing criticism by pleasing the people.

**Spiritual Abuse**

Generally, church people tend to trust their church leaders and sometimes this trust is abused by the leaders themselves. Because of their natural bent to that which "seems spiritual," many members become vulnerable to subtle ungodly treatments by leaders and others. Caution must be taken not to misuse or abuse anyone because of that person's spirituality.

To intentionally slander, discriminate, marginalize, undermine, conspire against persons and then without personal repentance, in the name of "Jesus," exhort, and admonish those same persons toward cooperation, forgiveness, brotherly love, and unity, holding that it is uncharacteristic of Christians to do otherwise, is taking advantage of these persons, mainly because of their spirituality.

*Spiritual abuse* is "When the idea of being spiritual is wrongly used to make a person live up to a so called 'spiritual standard' for the self-centered satisfaction of another person. This promotes external 'spiritual performance' . . . without regard to an individual's well-being." [1]

Christians who are privileged with church responsibilities must continually ask God for eye salve to ensure that they do not spiritually abuse those whom they are privileged to lead.

It is instructive to note Paul's counsel: "Let nothing be done through selfish ambition or conceit, but in lowliness of mind **let each esteem others better than himself**" (Philippians 2: 3, NKJV, emphasis applied).

Church people generally gravitate to whatever seems spiritual. There are many church leaders who use the concept of spirituality conveniently to suit their own desired outcome. A case in point is, if some church leaders wanting members to buy into their ideas, speak passionately about how spiritual their ideas are, but if those same ideas are raised by others, those same leaders speak of them as not being spiritually beneficial.

Also, some church leaders wrongly use the notion of spirituality to get compliance and cooperation on matters that are very controversial and clearly problematic. This use of the notion of spirituality is spiritual abuse.

**Actors**. Many church leaders are good actors regarding spirituality. For example, they will be present at many funeral services because of ulterior motives. They act as if they are spiritually touched to the point of tears and fainted voices, while in reality they are just trying to win for themselves the support of people.

There are many church leaders who do not go to church whenever they are not preaching or whenever they are on vacation. Some do not return tithe or offerings from income that are unknown by their organizations and at the same time they preach total faithfulness to their members. Some just focus on duties that they are paid to do but do not volunteer to help people outside of their job description and domain.

**Blind Victims**. Many leaders are apparently spiritual and religious but only when the time of election and appointment of church leaders is near. Outside of that time, they even call themselves names like "Hitler" and "the greatest church politicians of this time." Some really know that they are not spiritual but play the game. Others falsely believe they are the best example of Christ notwithstanding that they live contrary to the Christian faith, and are genuine blind victims of the church politics of their own mentors.

## Conclusive Spiritual Lessons

The problems of church politics pertaining to spirituality and religiosity encompass lack of conversion and a disconnect between spirituality and religiosity.

**Validation of Conversion.** "A form of godliness" without tapping into the power of spiritual resources must be turned away from. (See 2 Timothy 3:5). Jesus declares to Nicodemus "You must be born again" (St. John 3: 7 NKJV) and John the Baptist admonished the multitudes "Bear fruits worthy of repentance" (Luke 3: 8 NKJV). Church members look to church leaders for examples of Christlikeness. Validation of leaders' conversion is always under scrutiny.

The converted Christian has a genuine relationship with God which naturally bears the fruit of "Love joy, peace, longsuffering, kindness, goodness faithfulness, gentleness, self-control" (Galatians. 5: 22-23 NKJV). David prayed: "You desire truth in the inward being; therefore teach me wisdom in my secret heart. Purge me with hyssop, and I shall be clean" (Psalm 51: 6-7 NRSV).

Donald S. Whitney cites ten helpful questions to diagnose one's spiritual health:

1. Do you thirst for God?
2. Are you governed increasingly by God's word?
3. Are you more loving?
4. Are you more sensitive to God's presence?
5. Do you have a growing concern for the spiritual and temporal needs of others?
6. Do you delight in the Bride of Christ?
7. Are the spiritual disciplines increasingly important to you?
8. Do you still grieve over sin?
9. Are you a quicker forgiver?
10. Do you yearn for heaven and to be with Jesus?[2]

**Anchor Points**

Being spiritual, anchors the true meaning of being Christian and it is all about knowing Christ.

An actor after a brilliant performance of the twenty-third psalm received from his large audience a long standing ovation with tumultuous applause and shouts of satisfaction and approval of brilliance. Looking into the audience, the actor saw the pastor of his youth, the one who taught him the psalm. He wanted to hear it again from his teacher and therefore invited the old man on stage to say it for the audience. At the end of the old man's discourse, rather than applauding the audience broke into profuse tears.

The actor could not understand and to him the pastor explained: "You recited the psalm, I prayed the psalm; you know the words, I know the Shepherd."

True spirituality is all about knowing Christ and growing in Him!

# SPIRITUAL LESSONS FROM CHURCH POLITICS PERTAINING TO PREACHING

*"Every word of God is pure"*
(Proverbs 30: 5 NKJV).

W hat is the true purpose of preaching? Can preaching be misused to influence political outcomes? Are castigation, derision, lambasting, criticism viable causes or vicious curses of preaching?

## The Purpose and Power of Preaching

*Preaching* is the proclamation of the good news of God's grace. Good sermons are more than exhortation toward preparation for God's future kingdom; they are also social commentaries that impact minds and lives regarding the "here and now."

History is replete with powerful sermons which intercepted and impacted the path of bondage, spiritually and socially liberating countless people, helping them to understand and hold their grip on God, the supreme Liberator.

It is through preaching that church organizations are populated with people and church members keep growing spiritually in the face of moral decadence and social depravity.

Preaching is a powerful and spiritual exercise designed to effectively communicate God's will. Caution must be taken by preachers not to misuse this medium for personal gains.

## Self-Centered Preaching

The bull's eye of preaching is Christ, anyone or anything else is tangential.

**First Person's Orientation**. Many church leaders use preaching toward honoring themselves. They preach to be praised for it. They preach praising themselves regarding where they have been, what they have achieved, who they were with, how much they spent or did not have to spend because others spent it on them. In many cases God is but a miniature appendage in sermons dominated by self-praise. He is left out, left behind, and let down.

## Devotional Daggers

In some cases, church leaders have unresolved issues in their minds regarding fellow workers, and they use a devotional preaching opportunity to vent their disgust, losing out on a grand privilege to be Christlike.

They remain at, and wrongly use the altar "which they should leave and make it right with their brothers," and rather make it worse by offending them.

In exercises that are meant for worship, the true spirit of devotion to Christ is lost whenever the scriptures are twisted by preachers to curse, castigate, and condemn individuals for personal political reasons.

Devotional sermons are to help individuals to be more devoted to Christ. Church leaders who do not go the extra mile outside of the pulpit to solve their personal conflicts with fellow worshipers, are ethically and spiritually disqualified to be the same fellow worshipers' devotional spiritual instructors.

Conflicts and issues must be resolved by the biblical model dealing with your brother personally. Devotion is not a dagger to make wounds; it is a balm to heal sores. A good church culture creates an environment of proper neutral devotional worship service that heals after a conflict, not a service that perpetuates tension.

### Hermeneutical Malpractice

Many church leaders use preaching as means to mislead people conceptually on spiritual matters. They have ulterior motives regarding soliciting the people's support for their own biases.

Because they know how spiritually impressionable church people are pertaining to lessons from the Bible, these leaders in their preaching twist the interpretation of scriptures to fit their own biases and wrongly impress on the minds of their listeners, not just how God is but what He wants. This is hermeneutical malpractice toward unbiblical ends.

**Convenience.** Also some church leaders in their preaching use scriptures to support the election of their friends as leaders, identifying that these persons possess critical biblical leadership traits. Sometimes within a short time period, these same persons fall out of goodwill and then the same leaders who used scriptures to support these their then friends for leadership positions, now use other scriptures from the same Bible to condemn them, pointing out their bad characteristics.

**Illustrations.** Some preachers desperately seeking support for leadership positions fully make up or extensively inflated experiences about themselves or others whom they support, in order to influence or suppress individual choice.

## Conclusive Spiritual Lessons

Preaching is a sacred profession designed as God's audible voice of hope for a dying world. It is never to be used for personal selfish reasons, but to be, no more, or no less of what God says. The content of preaching ought always to be one hundred percent applicable to the person-medium through whom it is uttered.

**Personal Application**. The prophet Nathan proclaims to David a scenario of a rich man and a poor man who lived in a town. The rich man had many cattle and sheep and the poor man only had one sheep. The rich man had a guest and rather than killing one of his own sheep to provide a meal for his guest he sent for and killed the poor man's only sheep and the poor man's family went hungry. The question by Nathan to David was: "What must be done to this rich man?" David was furious and answered that the rich man must be put to death.

Nathan proclaimed in the context of David's sins in committing adultery with Uriah's wife and then technically murdering him at the battle front, "You are the one" (See 2 Samuel. 12: 1-13)

Preaching begins with the first person singular standing in the awesome sin-consuming presence of God. It ought also to end there with the divine declaration "well done, my good and faithful servant" (Matthew. 25: 21NLT).

**Sacrilegious Worship**. Dispute with one another must be settled face to face: "Leave your gift there before the altar and go your way. First be reconciled with your brother, and then come and offer your gift" (Matthew. 5: 24 NKJV). To use the pulpit to scold, curse, or reprimand your brother is sacrilegious. Moreover, in this worship context, more often than not, there is a strong counter response and sometimes with vehemence, but luckily based on respect for God, it is usually silent. In any case, the blessing of worship is lost and the preacher is less respected and the wound of dispute is deepened.

These preachers pass on to their intern pastors the bad practice of misusing preaching to abuse worshipers with whom they have unresolved conflicts. "What sorrow awaits the leaders of my people-the shepherds of my sheep-for they have destroyed and scattered the very ones they were expected to care for," says the LORD" (Jeremiah. 23: 1 NLT).

**Indispensable Preaching**. "Cry aloud, spare not: Lift up your voice like a trumpet; tell my people their transgression, and the house of Jacob their sins" (Isaiah. 58: 1 NKJV). Because the preacher is inclusive as "my people," the message is for him or her also. The preacher must genuinely land God's message toward application by the 1st person plural-"us." Consequently, the preacher is not the Master giving instruction but a mouthpiece taking and sharing instruction.

**Disclaimer.** A personal sermonic disclaimer in all situations is a helpful filter of motives for preaching. Here is an example: **"I take no responsibility or credit for your personal interpretation and application. This message is not meant to deride, castigate, lambast, nor in any way criticize anyone but only to generally motivate all toward a personal experience with Christ. I understand to do otherwise is to lose spiritual credibility."**

## Anchor Points

Whether at a church election session, post-election service, special convocation, or at a general church worship service, preaching that is based on proper biblical hermeneutics is indispensable for spiritual guidance pertaining to attitude and behavior regarding all church matters.

Preaching is sacred and must never be misused or abused because of personal ambition. Let God give you utterance and preach the word firstly to yourself and then proclaim the same to your other "selves"-people. Always remember the golden rule when preaching.

# SPIRITUAL LESSONS FROM CHURCH POLITICS PERTAINING TO SILENCE

*"A word fitly spoken is like apples of
gold in a setting of silver"*
(Proverbs 25: 11 ESV).

*"A time to keep silence, and
a time to speak"*
(Ecclesiastes 3: 7 NKJV).

What are some of the dangers of silence in the operations of church organizations? Is there ascending and descending liability for silence to wrongs in church work?

## The Sin of Silence

*Silence* is more than the absence of word sound, it is also the lack of action. Silence becomes very loud in church circles when blatant wrongs prevail in the presence of a mission of love and righteousness.

"All that is necessary for the triumph of evil is that good men do nothing" (Edmund Burke). The attitude of many church persons while wrong is predominant in the strata of their church hierarchy, is that good men must neither see nor hear any evil within their own religious organization, but certainly they must see evil and cry against it in the social and secular world.

## Trans-Regime Liability

Whether ecclesiastic or secular, every organization has its challenges. Sometimes these challenges include breach of ethics and violation of policy. In these cases, workers are usually at the disadvantage losing benefits, their resources, their job, and sometimes their pride.

These circumstances usually leave bitterness between church workers and church leaders who represent the church organization. Even when those guilty church leaders are off the scene, the bitterness of those workers remains against the organization itself.

**A New Regime.** In the same way that a new administrative regime in church organizations delights to inherit the assets of blessings, grandeur, resources, good name of the organization achieved by good leaders who preceded them, so are the liabilities equally transferred as the responsibility of the new administration of that organization. While generally speaking contractual arrangements made on behalf of church organizations by past church leaders, are usually honored by new church leaders, there seems to be a lack of interest to deal with the intangible liability of hurt to workers caused by previous administrative regimes.

History records apology of countries to countries they have wronged; church to people whom it had wronged, race to race whom it had wronged and in some cases with reparation although the apologizing leaders of these entities were bone long after the guilty leaders who oversaw the wrong committed.

**Choruses of Apology**. Church organizations which claim to be the bastion of purity, the vanguard of righteousness, and the model of relationship must go beyond liabilities of contractual bonds and break their silence in genuine choruses of apology to workers and others who have been hurt in the name of the organization. With this reformation what a revival would break out.

With this reformation, people with frowns will break out into laughter; persons who left the church will return with royal strides; people who moved their children to public schools will have them returned; members who withhold the tithe and offerings will write big checks; silent preachers will speak up; the engine of production will be revved up; more talents will be utilized; and the church will be revived.

In church organizations, new administrative regimes that are responsible, take liability for known hurts caused in the name of the organization, thereby demonstrating proper time of the end living.

## Shouts of Silence

As vanguards of brotherhood and citadels of right doing in the context of true love, church organizations must not take the vow of silence and perpetuate a culture of reticence on important issues whether it pertains to within the church or in society at large.

**Within the Church Organization**. If within a church organization there is a culture of silence based on fear, then that organization and its leaders need spiritual surgery and synergy.

Often times on some church committees, members who sit thereon, who in their inner most Bible-oriented souls, see something wrong in the leading and leaning of the Chair on particular matters, remain silent because of fear. What fear? The fear that it is going to appear that they are fighting against the program of the leader. Fear that subtle consequences at the hardened discretion of the leader sooner or later will be meted out to out-spoken committee members.

Many church leaders ensure that persons who are placed on administrative committees are those who are silent to the extent that the minority (few leaders) will determine the minds of the majority, hence perpetuating a culture of silence.

Within this culture of silence many church leaders lose credibility to cry out against the sins that affect the church in general, or on the other hand, hypocritically embrace double standards-its wrong for some persons but necessary for others.

*Committees without an official Chair.* Some church leaders cunningly act to keep silent the names of some church workers. In some cases these leaders take the praises that are rightly due to others. Some church leaders go to the extent of naming committees to do great tasks on behalf of the church but do not name an official Chair for these committees, but they ask competent persons to convene these committees and do the hard and technical work, but at the same time these persons' names are kept silent when the excellent outcomes are exhibited. In many cases main leaders unfairly takes the praise for themselves. According to the attitudes of these church leaders, nobody must hear the names of the persons who truly get the work done. Strangely enough, people always know the good works of others, and in these cases, silence shouts even after the persons' retirement. Is not to take another person's praise for one's self stealing and is not stealing of the Devil?

Also, some church leaders go far and wide paying much of the organization money to import presenters to deal with particular subjects pertinent to the growth of the organization while they could have utilized from among their own workers persons who are just as or even more competent than those imported. Why? Because many church leaders have ulterior motives for keeping home-based persons silent. These leaders concoct a lot of stories when the members ask "Why not use Sister X?"

**Toward Society in General.** Many church organizations have reneged on their calling to be God's mouthpiece regarding personal, communal, and national sin. They are more concerned to be cautious toward getting future benefits from society and its entities, including politician and governments. They are afraid and hide under the blanket of being "politically correct." Some churches expecting to get some credit hide behind other churches that "bawl out" against sins. Because of silence, sin is exalted and righteousness is seen as a reproach.

## Conclusive Spiritual Lessons

Silence is good for reverence, meditation, and analysis, but while "There is a time to keep silence . . . there is a time to speak" (Proverbs 3: 7 NKJV). David in his needs cried: "You have seen it, O LORD, do not keep silent" (Psalm. 35: 22 NASB). God declares: "For Zion's sake I will not keep silent, for Jerusalem's sake I will not remain quiet, till her righteousness shines out like the dawn, her salvation like a blazing torch" (Isaiah. 62: 1 NIV).

**God as Model.** People, directly or indirectly, whether they know it or not, are always in need for others to righteously speak on their behalf regarding decisions that will affect them. God has spoken out in more than words but also actions, the chief of which is the death of Jesus toward the salvation of the spiritually impoverished, destitute, and disenfranchised sinners who could not help themselves.

**Satan's Model**. An attempt to keep the righteous silent is Satan's model throughout time and church leaders must not be his accomplices. The consequence of Satan's model is eternal damnation.

**Time of the End Sign**. One of the signs of the time of the end is the sound of the Gospel by the church into all the world (Matthew 24). This is not an event; it is a lifestyle that permeates the value system of all believers. If it does not just affect the world but effects righteousness within the church itself, then how do we explain a culture of silence to sin within many church organizations?

## Anchor Points

"Cry aloud, spare not; lift up your voice like a trumpet; tell my people their transgression, and the house of Jacob their sins" (Isaiah. 58: 1 NKJV). This commission is an end time necessity.

Speaking out against sin must not be with the intent to embarrass, or hurt the sinner or the sinning organization, but at all times must be executed with a spirit of love toward redemptive transformation.

# SPIRITUAL LESSONS FROM CHURCH POLITICS PERTAINING TO PRAISE, PROMOTION, AND PUNISHMENT

*"Do not withhold good from those to whom it is due,
when it is in the power of your
hands to do so"*
(Proverbs 3: 27 NKJV).

Even though generally church organizations claim a structure of accountability, and a philosophy of equity and equality, can praise, promotion, and punishment be severely misused by church leaders?

## Organizational Psyche

Praise as motivation, promotion as reward, and punishment as penalty, are leadership responses to perceived or actual performance and behavior of church workers.

In the culture of any church organization, these three are prominent in the psyche of members, especially those who are employed in the grid of church leadership. The organizational psyche regarding praise, promotion, and punishment varies based on the prominence of practice within that particular church's culture itself.

## Perspectives on Praise

Praise directed to a person is satisfaction and appreciation regarding the person's performance. A Christian who is praised needs humility and a proper understanding of the earthly context of praise. Humility causes the person to be appreciative of compliment, but at the same time redirects all praises in thanksgiving to God.

**Praise as Life**. In the minds of many church persons maybe church leaders in particular, there seems to be a sort of "DNA" of praise that spurs performance. They walk to be praised; they dress to be praised; they accumulate possessions to be praised; they sing to be praised; they play musical instruments to be praised; they help people to be praised; they preach to be praised; they pray to be praised; they praise to be praised-praise is their life.

**Praise as Motivation**. Praise carefully conveyed as appreciation is motivational. It speaks to usefulness of an individuals' input, consequently people feel needed because they know that their doings are perceived as being beneficial to their organization. More praise as appreciation is needed in many church organizations despite the remuneration received by church workers for their services.

**Praise as Affirmation**. Praise for work done affirms that performance meets expectations. Consequently, workers are not left in doubt as to the fulfillment of their job description. There is the view that praise is like a cup filled with nutritious juice amid many persons who need these nutrients. But alas, there can be enough juice for everyone! More praise as affirmation is needed in many church organizations.

Praise must not be solicited, it must be voluntarily given affirming tasks as meeting expectations, and motivating workers to excellent services in God's work. At the same time all praises must be redirected to God.

## Self-Centered Praise

Many church organizations have adopted a strong culture of praise which is sometimes expressed through ceremonies. Certificates, citations, plaques, and insignias of recognition are built in the annual calendar of events and budget of many church organizations. When executed with pure motives, these ceremonies are reflective of true Christianity.

However, in many cases, praise, given publicly or privately, is not solely for the persons being praised, but it is done with ulterior motive with the ones to benefit being those doing the praising or awarding.

**First-time Syndrome**. First-time syndrome is the obsession of doing something for the first time and praising oneself for it. Many church leaders in quest of self-attention suffer from "first-time syndrome." They seek to over do things that are done for the first time and unnecessarily drawing people's attention to these things. These church leaders will even go to the extent of pointing out that they are the first ones to award so many workers, while the fact really is that their church worker force has grown numerically with time as compared with any past administrative period.

Sometimes it really appears that many church leaders award persons more for the sake of record and reporting than for the people themselves. First-time syndrome is a cry of lack of self-confidence by church leaders.

**Praise for Connections**. Church organizations are becoming increasing aware that to be relevant they must impact their communities. In many instances one of the ways the church connects with the community is through appreciation services. However, caution must be taken that this is not abused by awarding individuals merely for the sake of seeking long, medium, or short term benefits for the church organization, or its leaders. The people themselves must be the focus of the award they receive.

**Praise for Support**. Some church leaders sometimes only praise workers who give them political support. This support is usually directed to the gaining or retaining of powers by these leaders. At the same time, these same church leaders suppress and are silent regarding even more outstanding work done by other workers whose support toward gaining and retaining power is not guaranteed. Therefore, their praise is more for self-benefit.

Praising people for the purpose of getting support from them can be blatantly seen in many church circles. Consequently, only individuals who hold strategic elected positions are awarded although others not in these positions have impacted unique areas of church life within the organization's territory. The culture of praise for support in some church organizations can blind the eyes of church leaders to being pure and genuine with praise.

## Perspectives on Promotion

Promotion more often than not is the concept of vertical motion on the church's organizational work hierarchy, although to some extent it can be horizontal on a particular level. Whatever it is, this movement generally comes with more benefits within the grid of resources, opportunities, power, and prestige.

Generally, in church organizations, good performance and adequate qualification in the face of opportunity and vacancy are important factors favoring promotion. While it is known that everybody will not necessarily be promoted, people generally desire promotion.

Consequently, many church workers obey the codes of conduct of their organizations, perform exceptionally well at their jobs, and furthermore qualify themselves for the possibility of a job at a so-called "higher" level and wait patiently for this opportunity, not so much to benefit themselves, but to build up the work the Lord has entrusted to His church.

In each promotion of persons, the promotion of the Lord's work must be critically considered. How will these persons take the work asked to do to a higher level?

## Promotional Pitfalls

Generally, in church organizations promotion mainly comes by election or appointment, depending on the type and level of promotion.

The process of election is already discussed in earlier chapters. The process of appointment has many pitfalls, especially when church leaders derail the process of proper procedures in order to benefit themselves.

**Hand-picked Committees**. Appointments are usually done either directly by main church leaders or through committees hand-picked by the leaders themselves. In many cases, these committee members are chosen merely because they will confirm the leader's choice without being critically objective. The process is misused to fulfill the leaders' biases, sometimes to the detriment of the work of God.

Consequently, the process of promotion is not always fair and transparent. People who are best qualified and who are savvy with the organizational culture are not always chosen, but those less qualified and have poor work ethic are promoted as means toward selfish ends.

**Meaningless Interviews**. Sometimes, although church leaders preselect particular persons to fill vacant positions, in order to let the process appear to be fair, these same positions are advertised and several interviews conducted. In these cases, being shams, these interviews are but a waste of time and resources.

In these manners some church leaders abuse their power and promote whomsoever they desire. Promotions must be transparent and fair, especially within church organizations which claim to be bastions of righteousness.

Conditions for promotion must be clearly documented and presented to workers at all levels of church organization. Ongoing assessment and evaluation of all workers including top church leaders must be done, and discussed in an appropriate context.

## A Punishment Mindset

While in church organizations penalty ought to merely be the natural outcome of violation of established agreements between the organization and its workers, some church leaders go overboard because of their punishment mindset, and lean toward hurting in one way or another, the violators, especially those who they do not consider their friends.

In this punishment mind-set context, workers must never be in ignorance regarding the precise expected consequences of particular violations. The church's codes of conduct must be presented and discussed whenever individuals are interviewed toward being employed by a church organization. Agreement to this must be demonstrated by signatures of the new workers. Therefore, in the minds of all workers there will be a consciousness of codes of conduct and their associated consequences if violated.

### Power and Punishment

Many church leaders rather than even following their organization's codes of conduct in relation to discipline and penalty, become obsessed with their power, wrongly using it toward their personal biases.

**Unlimited Power**. Many church leaders demote, suspend, withdraw benefits from, and dismiss workers unconstitutionally and illegally based on their personal dislike of those individuals. Many church workers who are dealt with unfairly by church leaders, because of the notion that Christians do not take their church dispute to the secular courts, take their hurt without contest. Because of this, some church leaders seem to have unlimited power.

**Dispute Resolution Boards**. Many dispute resolution boards set up by the church, more often than not, when church leaders are the subjects of dispute with workers, rule in favor of those church leaders. Also, some dispute resolution boards when relating to dispute among workers do approach the matter with favoritism and tend to lean on the side taken by church leaders. Consequently, in some church circles, justice is not generally seen in judgments, and mercy though uncommon, is associated with being "too soft-hearted."

**Double Standards.** Many unconverted church leaders use their power to badly hurt violators of the organization's codes of conduct, yet overlook the violation of their supporters; they treat minor offences as major ones only in relation to workers not considered their friends. At the same time, their friends' major offences are treated as minor ones or as nothing at all. Double standards reign in many church organizations.

## Conclusive Spiritual Lessons

Regarding praise, promotion, and punishment meted out to church workers, equality, equity, and grace are indispensable to God-centered church governance.

**Big Impression but Little Respect**. Some church leaders who focus on doing things solely to make an impression on the larger society, sometimes from their own people, lose the respect of being genuine and sincere leaders. Many of these leaders are very unhappy whenever they are not praised especially in details. Some of these leaders resort to praise their own selves. "A man's pride brings him low, but a man of lowly spirit gains honor" (Proverbs 29: 23 NIV).

**Equity and Equality**. "Do not withhold good from those to whom it is due, When it is in the power of your hands to do so" (Proverbs 3: 27 NKJV). Church leaders must not seek to give workers less than they deserve and at the same time all persons though having different portfolios, must be respected as being of equal worth. Praise and promotion that are based on equity and equality enhance belonging, human dignity, and a positive work environ.

**As He Deserved**. "This is what the LORD Almighty says: 'Administer true justice; show mercy and compassion" (Zechariah. 7: 9 NIV). Remember "Christ was treated as we deserve, that we might be treated as He deserves."[1]

Church leader must not think punishment but discipline toward correcting the shortcomings of workers in order to better their future.

### Anchor Points
Without the grace of God there is nothing praiseworthy about anyone, and consequently nothing

worthy of promotion, and everything justifiable of the punishment of eternal death (See Romans. 6: 23).

Giving praise and promotion is a spiritual matter which must be joyfully executed, bearing in mind the supreme price Jesus placed on every human being. Receiving praise and promotion ought to be a humbling spiritual experience which does not absorb praise and promotion to one's heart but channels this in thanksgiving to God.

Justifiable punishment or consequence must be executed with mercy, and at the same time must be accepted without rancor or malice bearing in mind that the worst punishment is to miss out on heaven.

# SPIRITUAL LESSONS FROM CHURCH POLITICS PERTAINING TO POLICY, PROCEDURE, AND PROTOCOL

*"Let all things be done decently and in order"*
(1 Corinthians. 14:40 NKJV).

Wvhat are the purposes of policy, procedure, and protocols in the operations of church organizations? Are they always necessary? How are they wrongly used by some church leaders for their personal benefits?

## Organizational Guides

A *policy* is an agreed upon, and an officially accepted organizational administrative guideline predicated on a principle of consistency, toward guarding against imposition, impropriety, and injustice. A policy is generally issue based.

*Procedure* is a linear concept. It pertains to the sequence of events to properly follow, and by whom, in the conduct of the business of the organization, whether it pertains to conducting meetings, or in effecting decisions.

*Protocol* concerns precedence and titles relative to hosting, addressing, and generally relating to people of various classes and positions in life.

## Policy as Secret

In many cases, church organizational policies seem to be the personal properties of elected leaders, and sometimes these policies appear to be the orders of a somewhat secret society. Though printed as books, policies in many cases are only available to the elected leaders. Policies in parts are occasionally presented at some church meetings as leaders' reaction to particular church issues. In these cases, so-called "policy-expert-leaders" communicate to the attendees, their unilateral interpretations of these policies.

In some cases, toward affecting the biases of the church leaders, these so-called "experts" only present and interpret parts of many policies pertaining to the same issue. In some churches, trained workers and lay persons alike who want to examine the full policy book, cannot even borrow it overnight from their church organizations, but have to use it within limited time at their church headquarters. Moreover, in some church organizations, the idea of workers' wanting to see the policy book arouses in the minds of church leaders, suspicion that these workers are against their administration. Also, at times workers who show vested interest in organizational working policies are believed to be planning an overthrow of that current church administration.

In this information age, should not all church workers at least those employed to their church organization, have at their disposal, the policies that guide how they are governed? Some organizations give workers an annual updated booklet of changes to salaries and emoluments. While this is good and usable, they are not policies encompassing the deeper, wider, and weightier matters to unravel issues.

**Keeping the Policy Oral**. Some organizations are more advanced than others to the extent that they have presentations of their working polices to their employees at least annually. A forum is created for dialogue and clarification, especially when there are organizational policy changes. However, in some of these church organizations, the policy is always kept oral pertaining to the people while the leaders have it in written form.

**Denied for Lack of Knowledge**. When many of these same employees though educated on the policies orally are nominated to serve as leaders, the argument that they lack knowledge pertaining to the working policies is used toward disqualifying them. Implicitly, oral education is not believed to be enough.

Why would a church organization keep its working policies only oral to the workers in general but make the same policies available in written form to church leaders? The argument of printing cost is untenable because the policy can be made available electronically. Furthermore, cannot certification in organizational policy be offered and credited as continuing education? And moreover many continuing education credits in some church organizations are repeats of what workers already know.

## Policy as a Divider

A policy especially in relation to any true Christian organization is supposed to unite not divide workers. A critical motif of any church policy is a proactive resolution to actual and potential issues. It is to manifest justice and fairness.

While policy makers within church organizations must design policies that bear in mind national and regional government policies pertaining to race, class, or rank, all church policies must have Christlikeness as the main point of reference. In this Christ is glorified.

Policies that are based on hierarchy and not on qualifications, years of service, or performance, probably increase political maneuvering for leadership positions.

If a church policy supports a church leader's salary, fringe benefits, and retirement benefits being substantially higher than a committed counterpart with the same qualifications and years of service, but who only does not hold a leadership position at that level, is this policy Christlike?

If a church policy supports inequality of human beings based on nationality, race, class, or ethnic group, is it Christlike?

If church policy makers change policies to benefit themselves depending on where they are in their journey of their organizational life, is it Christlike?

If church leaders firmly adhere to policies pertaining to some workers and ignore these same policies regarding other workers whom they see as their friends and assets to their gaining and retaining power, are those leaders not abusing church policies for political reasons?

## Procedure as God's Nature

Procedure must be adopted and followed in Christian organizations engendering order that is consistent and comprehensive. God is a being of order. From the minutest of atoms to the largest organism; from the order of heaven with archangel to the organization of the Early Church with overseers; and greater still the important roles each member of the Godhead carries out in the history of salvation, all testify to the fact that God operates in supreme order.

## Procedure and Chairmanship

**Christian Procedure**. Historically, Christian organizations adopted rules of order that were meant to facilitate and enhance the proper conduct of church meetings on behalf of the Lord Himself. Proper procedure is not only having the proper sequence of actions regarding how an issue or point is raised, discussed, and acted upon, but it anchors critical Christian values of morality and ethics displayed in these sequences.

**Mental Processing**. If a person allows a sinful thought counter to God's work to proceed to be spoken publicly whether on a committee or before a larger body of believers, then that is a reflection of a serious moral glitch in mental processing. That immoral thought should have been intercepted and destroyed by stronger Christlike thoughts, as "goodness is stronger than evil." Furthermore, in that context, the chairman of that meeting has the procedural autonomy to disallow it. Proper mental processing of morality sets the stage for proper procedure of order pertinent to conducting the church's business through a committee etc.

**Double Standards**. A Christian chairman must ensure that the procedure of the meeting is follows a Christian manner and content. If a chairman instructs the members of a committee not to speak evil of anyone who is being discussed and yet that chairman personally does otherwise, it is a double standard.

Also, if a chairman allows only some members to participate orally, that is double standard. If a chairman commands and threatens a board toward supporting a particular point or person, that is way below Christian standards and is very unethical.

**Ascending Liability**. Most church organizations have clear ranks of administrations. Higher ranks of administrations must ensure that those on the lower levels adhere to proper procedures. Whenever people of higher administrations allow those on the lower levels to blatantly in their very presence violate procedures in order to fulfill their own desires, the persons of higher organizations have failed to do their job and must take full responsibility for those actions. When procedures break down, members lose faith in all levels of the church.

## Procedure and Action

Church leaders must think of procedure from the perspective of protecting their organizational integrity. Proper procedure not only leaves a clear, genuine, and professional path of the past but gives a precedence of guidance for the future. Leaders come and leaders go but the organization remains. "Let those who come behind you find you faithful."

**Selectivity**. In taking actions or carrying out decisions, church leaders must not be inconsistent, partial, and selective. They must be consistent. In many church organizations the practice of breaching procedure is very evident pertaining to both internal and external matters. At times church leaders breach procedure in regard to administration within the church, but are very firm on procedure in relating to the outside world and vice a versa. In many cases because of political reasons, church organizational procedures are breached by overstepping appropriate people, circumnavigating essential board actions, and by making tit-for-tat prominent.

**Appointment, Employment, and Dismissal**. Every church organization has to deal with appointment, employment, and to a lesser extent dismissal of workers.

There must be transparency in the appointment and employment of workers in church organizations. Many church leaders in the quest to appoint and employ their friends and relatives violate proper procedures by passing over at times the persons most qualified for the job.

Regarding dismissal, many church leaders violate procedure in technically dismissing workers whom they believed are not important to them for political mileage. Many church leaders in an effort to unfairly dismiss some workers cite reasons that are not tenable and substantial to merit dismissal. In some cases they trick many workers into believing that there is adequate basis for dismissal and claiming that they the leaders are merciful, and are advising the workers to take special leave. Rather than educating themselves with the Labor Laws of their country, state or county and the working policy and procedures of their church organization, these workers resign or take leave to the fulfillment of their employers' political craftiness.

There are genuine cases in which good church leaders are really graceful to workers. But many church leaders do not fall into that good category; they violate procedures and laws to dismiss workers for political and personal reasons. Also, many church leaders seem happy when some workers fall into sin and merit dismissal, they quickly follow organizational procedure and dismiss them but without exit counsel.

**Procedural Abuse**. If a chairman calls for the vote of those who constitutionally must decide what the church organization does on any particular matter, but refuses to count the votes notwithstanding that it is a close call, because he wants to have it his way, he is apparently using the power of the chair to highjack the people's right. In this case procedure is breached.

## Protocol as Reflection of Perception

True protocol is a gesture of respect for people in important ranks of service that are important to be recognized and highlighted.

Many church leaders are very concerned and sometimes overly obsessed about protocol but only in so far as it relates to hosting and addressing dignitaries from outside the church community. Protocol is also very much relevant when relating to people within church organizations. Ranks of service are not only evident in the secular world but are prominent in church organizations. While some church leaders try to get the proper titles and order of precedence for others correctly, they treat those of their own organizations as people without class, failing to use protocol in relating to their fellow workers on and below their leadership level, but at the same time they are very protocol minded in relating to their church superiors and state officials.

Each church organization must build a strong inter and intra protocol culture. Consequently, whenever people, irrespectively of their ranks as state officials or as members of other institutions, are hosted by that church organization, they will have a good sense of "the greatest work on earth" of carrying the gospel of salvation to sinful beings and the church's respect for the different people who carry it, and those to whom it is carried.

## Conclusive Spiritual Lessons

Order constitutes the very nature of God. The physical and chemical balance of the universe are all based on principles ordained of God. God wisely gave laws as policies to keep society in check and most importantly to keep humanity spiritually healthy. With protocol implications the Bible advises: "Give respect and honor to those who are in authority" (Romans. 13: 7 NLT).

**No Exception.** Although God commanded that all Jewish male children must be circumcised, Moses the prophet did not circumcise his own son and God himself "was about to kill him. But Zipporah took a flint knife, cut off her son's foreskin and touched {Moses'} feet with it. "Surely you are a bridegroom of blood to me," she said. So the LORD let him alone" (Exodus. 4: 24-25 NIV).

Church policies and procedures based on God's principles must be affirmed and consistently applied without favoritism. "To show partiality is not good" (Proverbs 28: 21 NIV).

## Anchor Points

God did not change the principle of the natural consequence of sin. He paid a high or great price through the death of His only begotten Son Jesus. In so doing the requirements of justice were met and at the same time, mercy was extended to whosoever will.

Because of His own principled nature He could not change the law to suit Himself. He followed the procedure of the sacrificial system and as the Lamb of God He replaced the earthly lamb as its antitype. He taught with protocol implications: "Render to Caesar the things that are Caesar's, and to God the things that are God's" (Mark 12: 17 KJV).

# SPIRITUAL LESSONS FROM CHURCH POLITICS PERTAINING TO PRIVACY AND PUBLICITY

*"Thy Father which seeth in secret shall reward thee openly"*
(Matthew 6: 6 KJV).

*"I will not remember your sins"*
(Isaiah 43: 25 NKJV).

W hat is the politics of privacy and publicity? Can private or public matters in church governance be politicized? What appropriate lessons of privacy and publicity can be learnt from Christ's sacrifice on Calvary's Cross?

## Spectrum of Privacy and Publicity

Privacy is the opposite of publicity. Publicity is the reality of accessibility to information, events, and matters pertaining to a person or a body of people such as a class, a school, a church, a committee or council, a department in a company, a company itself, a community, a country etc. On the other hand, privacy confines information making it only accessible to particular persons.

## Dealing with Disagreement

In George Orwell's book Animal Farm, Molly the mule was created as equals with the other animals until she became the leader, or so she thought.[1] Many church leaders in relation to privacy and publicity behave as if they are not equal to other church workers but instead are superior. They announce their particular achievements publicly, but on the other hand, if they do, they announce the same success of other workers only privately.

**Public Monologue**. It seems inevitable that there will be disagreements between leaders and other church workers. When disagreement occurs, some church leaders use their position of power to publicly defend themselves, sometimes with vehemence, while at the same time, the side of those who are not privileged with voice within that public forum, is never heard.

**Private Dialogue**. Some church leaders publicly reprimand even their fellow officers causing them public embarrassment. Many times the cause for that situation results from the short comings of the reprimanding leaders themselves. Because of Christian principle of not washing dirty linen in public, those reprimanded workers do not publicly expose the reprimanding leaders' short coming. In private one to one dialogue, some leaders acknowledge their error in their public outburst and lack of information. They apologize only in private, but they never do so publicly, and the public belief that the other person was wrong, never dies even after the person's death.

## Disciplining of Workers

In many church organizations whenever discipline is executed on members/workers who are believed to have violated the code of ethics etc, often times many church administrators seek to protect those members/workers by not bringing the details of the violation to the public domain, especially if it is an embarrassing liability to the organization or those persons. Furthermore, in many cases the person in violation is gracefully given the option to voluntarily resign rather than being dismissed by the organization. That is Christlikeness.

**Silent Abuse of Secrecy**. However, in many other cases some church leaders have workers resign or have been dismissed on the basis of mere allegations. When pressed by other workers for an explanation for why these workers are forced to resign or dismissed, these church leaders claim that the situation is so bad that they rather be silent in order to protect the workers. While the truth is, for political reasons they capitalize on, and intentionally unjustly over-emphasize a controllable situation. In this case the notion of secrecy is abused on the premise of silence, and the innocent without a fair trial is found guilty.

**Audible Abuse of Secrecy**. On the other hand, there are cases when workers have clearly violated organizational code of conduct and merit dismissal. In those cases, enough must be said to preserve confidence to safeguard the integrity of the organization, and at the same time, no more than sufficient must be revealed to protect the workers. This delicate balance is indispensable to proper church governance.

Some church leaders publicly reveal unnecessary details of the violation of workers and at the same time they say "keep it private, do not tell anyone," when in truth they really want the details to be told to the extent of further hurting and devastating those workers. Is that behavior Christlike?

## Conclusive Spiritual Lessons

God made him who had no sin to be sin for us, so that in him we might become the righteousness of God" (2 Corinthians 5: 21 NIV). God through Jesus Christ our Lord and Savior has borne the public blunt of shame for our sin. At the same time he covers our nakedness and faults with his righteousness. Herein lies heaven's principle of publicity and privacy in which God is impartial in publicly covering our private defects with the justifiable price of His own blood.

## Anchor Points

God will defend the righteous from the secret plots of the Devil as is recorded in Psalm 64: 3-7 (NLT):

> *"They sharpen their tongues like swords*
> *and aim their bitter words like arrows.*
> *They shoot from ambush at the innocent,*
> *attacking suddenly and fearlessly.*
> *They encourage each other to do evil*
> *and plan how to set their traps in secret.*
> *"Who will ever notice?" they ask.*
> *As they plot their crimes, they say,*
> *"We have devised the perfect plan!"*
> *Yes, the human heart and mind are cunning.*
> *But God himself will shoot them with his arrows,*
> *suddenly striking them down."*

# SPIRITUAL LESSONS FROM CHURCH POLITICS PERTAINING TO FRIENDSHIP

*"The righteous should choose his friend carefully,*
*for the way of the wicked leads them astray"*
(Proverbs 12: 26 NKJV).

*"There are "friends" who destroy each other,*
*but a real friend sticks closer than*
*a brother"*
(Proverbs 18: 24 NLT).

What is true Christian friendship? Is there a place for friendship in the work of God although church relations are based on brotherhood? Can friendship between some violate brotherhood toward others?

## True Friendship

True *friendship* is a bond of allegiance between two or more persons who find joy and commonality in being in one another's presence.

In the Christian faith, people based on being together in historical, circumstantial, and common contexts, tend to naturally bond, some to a great degree resulting into friendship. Friendship has to be reciprocally nourished in order to survive and grow to a deep level of commitment. Christian brotherhood and sisterhood relationship is based on an understanding and acceptance of the fatherhood of God. Although Christians are brothers and sisters without necessarily truly knowing and bonding with each other, technically, their relationship, whenever it is Christ-centered is at a higher, deeper, and wider level than mere friendship.

At the same time, whenever true friends are Christian brothers or sisters, this relationship is unique and special, and spiritual caution must be taken, that an earthly friendship does not negatively affect heavenly brotherhood.

*Circumstantial Friendship.* Some relational bonds are merely based on circumstances of need, and must not be mistaken for friendship. For example a person might over time use much effort, means, and time to do something important and personally beneficial for a church leader, but it does not mean that the church leader takes that person as a friend and consequently will defend or go the extra mile for that person. Some relations are mistaken as true friendships although they are just based on temporal circumstances. These relations cease as early as the circumstance of benefits etc become non-existent.

In church work many persons do favors for church leaders only because they are expecting some present or future favors in return. At the same time, some church leaders befriend persons who can help them along their journey of progress. In many cases, thee church leaders are not even interested in the progress of those who help to make them progressive. True friendship is not based on self-benefits but commitment to giving ones' self.

## Position-Based Friendship

Many church leaders who have no historical acquaintance with each other, believe that being similarly appointed or elected to church leadership positions, makes them instant friends. Consequently, their introduction of each other becomes prefaced with "My good friend X."

**Leaders Who are Voted "Out."** This friendship is embarrassingly tested whenever some of these same high and mighty church leaders are not voted back into their leadership office and therefore are in need of a so-called good placement in the work. In many cases, their so-called friends (circumstantial) who remain in leadership positions, say and do nothing favorable on their behalf. One church leader, who did not get his desired job, described his state as an animal tied out to eat grass and forgotten by his circumstantial friends. In another church organization, a leader not voted back into his position pleaded "Don't treat me as a friend, just love me as a brother."

In many cases, these leaders who are not voted back into office are suddenly seen as liability to their "friends" who remain in office. In this context, those who remain in office believe that they will jeopardize themselves if they try to help their position-based circumstantial friends. Sometimes some church leaders really want to help their "friends" but are afraid of the wider worker force's negative reaction. If church leaders who remain in office had a good trust worthy relationship with the workers, more often than not there would be no negative reaction to fear because respected and well treated workers are generally respectful and accommodative.

**Leaders Who are Voted In**. Also, in many Christian organizations, many leaders who are voted into church office suddenly but intentionally forget their historical friends relating to them only as fellow professionals.

Sometimes leaders who are voted into office psychologically want their superiors to affirm them as being worthy of the job to which they have been elected, go over board to prove themselves as firm and impartial disciplinarians.

Consequently, they see their ideal validating test of firmness and impartiality, as their ability to discipline their "believed-to-be-friends." This type of church leader waits anxiously, watches keenly, and listens attentively, desiring a case to hurt the "believed-to-be-friends" in order to gain the respect of church superiors. Many are very disappointed when their "believed-to-be-friends" remain efficient workers and loyal servants to the organization.

**Relationships between church leaders not voted back into church offices and those who replace them**: In many church organizations there is at times, a spirit of animosity and division among leaders who are not voted back into office and those who replace them. In some cases hate language is used by these leaders or by their supporters to describe the relationship of these two groups.

In an effort to prove that the relationship at least on one side, has no semblance of friendship, but is one of great divide and bitterness, the voted in leaders, assign the hardest and most remote tasks to the voted out leaders. While the vindictive leader ask "Why not?", the Christlike asks "Why?"

## Compromise and Friendship

Spiritual leaders are expected to be able to clearly differentiate between righteousness and sin, right and wrong and, humility and arrogance. A true Christian friend does not cover up sin, wrong, or arrogance on the pretense of friendship.

Some church leaders are not really spiritual. For them position and power are more important than doing what is moral and right. They support their friends' wrong doing, but at the same time are quick to rebuke and condemn the mistakes of other workers who are not considered their friends.

**Opportunity Lost**. Many church leaders as they climb the leadership ladder from one level of administration to another do so with great leadership shortcomings and sometimes moral defects. People are usually most receptive to their friends. Friends who are the best ones to objectively and honestly point out leadership defects and moral defaults in church leaders, seem in many instances to cast a blind eye compromising the right and missing golden opportunities to correct these serious problems. Consequently, these church leaders are not helped, their problems intensify and perpetuate, embarrassing the church organization and results in increasing disrespect for church leaders generally.

Sometimes when an arrogant church leader is voted out of office and needs to learn humility as a regular church pastor, his lesson of humility is aborted by a friend on the higher level of the church organization who extends to him a call to save face. So instead of learning the lesson of humility to make him a better leader he is rewarded with a position in the upper echelon of the church organization. He never learns the lessons of humility and sometimes uses his position as a platform to exact revenge against those he felt were responsible for his removal from leadership.

Tenure of service in some church organizations spans 40 years before retirement. Some church leaders give 40 years of disrespectful, arrogant, and vindictive service to their church organizations and have never been helped by their friends to be otherwise. On the other hand, many church leaders with these tendencies have been helped by their friends.

Church leaders who claim that they are friends must not fail to correct one another regarding leadership shortcomings and moral glitches, because this failure potentially has serious organizational consequences.

Christian friends must help one another grow spiritually and morally. A person who compromises the truth lacks the mettle of true friendship.

## Blind Friendship

I heard it said that there are three types of friends: Friends whom you help; friends with whom you reciprocate help; and friends from whom you expect help. Generally, in most church organizations, friendship involves, "helping" in one way or another.

In relation to church leadership positions, quite often friendship is based on how a person can benefit by getting a position in church leadership. In some church organizations, many people behave lower than their self-worth to become close together, because if they do not, the church culture is that they will "perish." So it is believed. To a great extent so it is in reality in many church organizations.

There is good sense in people bonding together as friends. However, in the Christian context, caution must be taken to ensure that other church workers who are not in one's circumference of friendship, are not seen as enemies resulting in animosity and hatred being developed toward them.

In many church organizations people who do not have the requisite competencies and skills are placed in church leadership positions solely on the basis of friendship. Friends help friends to the detriment of the work of God. Friendship must not be blind to what is best for the work of God.

## Teams of Friendship

In some church organizations, being elected to the top leadership position on any particular administrative level, the leader is privileged to advise and plead to the nominating committee for his or her friends to be placed filling critical positions in the Administration.

Forming an administrative team from previous friendship has negative implications for a church that is based on Christian brotherhood and sisterhood. This culture polarizes the church on the premise of friendship.

There must be brotherhood for God's cause first, and friendship for social life second. Sometimes a church leader wants "friendship" not for mere team cohesion but for partnership in covering tracks of wrongs, one of which is financial impropriety.

Also, teams of friendship are not necessarily derived from pervious friendships but can be developed among team members who have been placed to work together based on competencies. In any case friendship must never support that which is not Christian in its nature.

## Conclusive Spiritual Lessons

Friendship within the Christian community is strengthening to the Christian life:

1. "You adulterous people, don't you know that friendship with the world is hatred toward God? Anyone who chooses to be a friend of the world becomes an enemy of God" (James 4:4 NIV).

2. "The righteous should choose his friend carefully, for the way of the wicked leads them astray" (Proverbs 12: 26 NKJV).

3. "Such wicked people are detestable to the LORD, but he offers his friendship to the godly" (Proverbs 3: 32 NLT).

4. "Make no friendship with an angry man, and with a furious man do not go" (Proverbs 22: 24 NKJV).

5. "The friendship of the LORD is for those who fear him, and he makes known to them his covenant" (Psalm 25: 14 ESV).

## **Anchor Points**

Specific bond of friendship between some persons must never be valued above the common bond of brotherhood between all persons.

"So in everything, do to others what you would have them do to you" (Matthew 7: 12 NIV).

# SPIRITUAL LESSONS FROM CHURCH POLITICS PERTAINING TO DISCIPLESHIP

*"You are my disciples"*
(John 13: 35 NLT).

W hat is true discipleship? Should church leaders have disciples like Christ did? Can Christian mentorship or internship be endangered by a human's quest for personal followers?

## True Christian Discipleship

True *Christian discipleship* is the disciplining of one's self in the character values modeled by Christ. This leads to a sustained compulsion to educate others and model to them what it means to follow Christ.

The disciplined member through divine help in following Christ reflects His character and participates in His commission to go into the entire world as witnesses of His grace. Church leaders irrespective of their positions are not divinely commissioned as masters to be followed but as fellow servants to follow God, the true Master of all Christian disciples.

## Followers of the Fallible

One of the serious problems in many church organizations is that several church leaders want to have their own disciples. These church leaders build a network of followers of mostly younger workers who are loyal to them to the extent that these followers compromise Christian values some of which are truthfulness, respect for all persons, and reverence for sacred entities.

**Power Factor**. Many church leaders by their attitudes and words impress on the minds of workers that they the leaders have leadership power enough to guarantee followers power of their own through church office, now and in the future. Followers who desire power through church leadership positions, are susceptible to follow men for this power and thereby are prone to become false disciples following earthly leaders who are all fallible.

**Manner of Life Factor**. In some circles, many workers follow their earthly church leaders as their masters, not just by value-compromising loyalty, but also by mannerisms, gestures, vocal expressions, attire, and generally ways of life.

**Conceptual Factor**. Also, there is the discipleship that is based on concepts that drive attitudes. In this case, followers become reflectors of the philosophies and world views of the church leader whom they follow. Sometimes these concepts run counter to democracy and the work of the Holy Spirit in church operations.

## Over Stepping Toward Discipleship

Most Christian organizations for their survival and growth depend on the most senior generation of leaders to pass on the baton of leadership to the next generation. This act is based on the premise that all other things being equal, knowledge and wisdom peculiar to each organization, come with experience which increases with years of quality service.

Each generation passes to the next generation essential lessons of leadership. It is the general practice for a person from the generation with the most experience to be elected as the top leader at each administrative level. There are some exceptions based on the mitigating circumstances such as massive disasters claiming the lives of senior leaders, organizational systemic problem in properly training of leaders, or lack of vision in systematically employing enough leaders over time, hence the lack of enough competent and available leaders in each generation.

Here is the political problem: many leaders who oversee important levels of administration, desire to prolong their own tenure of leadership positions at a very high level, therefore they seek to make their own disciples. In so doing, they radically skip the more experienced leaders preferring less experienced ones solely for political reasons. To do so, these top level leaders orchestrate and craftily plot the outcome of elections or appointments of these less experienced persons. Usually, in this case, the work of the Lord is spiritually stalled.

More often than not, these leaders who rise to power in the preceding manner become disciples to their masters, the higher leaders who put them there. While some of these younger leaders through their conversion to Christ and humility of spirit do very well in handling power and authority, the majority seem to be bossy, dictatorial, and arrogant in carrying out their earthly master's will. Therefore, in many cases the earthly church 'masters' rule above the people's will, through these their disciples.

## Interns for Christ or
## Disciples of Men?

Church organizations on the whole have an internship program where newly employed workers are placed to understudy an experienced worker. This experienced person acts as advisor and guide in technical wisdom and practical skills.

This advisor is to mentor these inexperienced workers regarding the ethos of the church, the proper execution of their job, and at the same time model Christ to them. Through this means essential knowledge is passed on progressing and growing the organization making vital contributions to its mission.

Internship and mentorship programs are meant to refine disciples of Christ not to make disciple-loyalists for church leaders themselves. Many church leaders misuse and abuse the privilege of having interns whom their organization has invested into their care. Rather than making these interns good disciples of Christ, many church senior leaders corrupt their minds regarding their organization and work, and furthermore distort their views of God.

Whenever internship and mentorship programs are abused toward self-exaltation of senior church leaders, the church organization has suffered by a breach that is spiritual, professional, and ethical.

In Christian internship or mentorship encounter, Christ is to be the focus, His standard the ideal, and His goal for His children heavenly. On the other hand, in human discipleship, the competence, knowledge, and manner of life of the church leader wrongly become the ideal points at which the intern reaches crescendo.

**Dependence.** Many church leaders engender a spirit of dependence in the minds of their interns. Therefore, many interns because of lack of conversion to Christ and greed for earthly status become dependent on their senior church leaders for benefits encompassing power, privilege, knowledge, and resources including money. Consequently, beyond the stipulated organizational internship period, many workers remain "intern-disciples" for the life period of their seniors. They are never weaned.

**Obligation**. Some senior church leaders foster from their interns a spirit of personal obligation. Therefore, many interns feel obligated to senior church leaders who explain church policy regarding benefits to workers. Church policies are not meant to be kept as secrets. All employees have the right to know the policies pertinent to employment. Whatever the benefits are, great or small, interns are not obligated to senior church leaders because these church leaders make known a benefit based on organizational policy.

Also, if a senior church leader teaches the intern to do something or donate something or a money to the intern, the intern must be appreciative but not to the extent of feeling obligated and to be a follower or disciple of that senior leader. Appreciation in internship or mentorship must be void of obligation. Obligation can lead to organizational slavery.

## Obligation by Location

Many church leaders know that positive influence on any problem group is maximized whenever that group is taken even for a short time from their environment to a new controlled environment—camps and retreats are examples of these.

Some church leaders wrongly use this foregoing concept toward political ends. These leaders believe that merely taking church workers to a retreat, a new country or a place, exposing them to new experiences, and somewhat brainwashing them, psychologically impact them resulting in obligatory loyalty–disciples of men. It does work but only relative to the caliber of church workers.

## Conclusive Spiritual Lessons

D iscipleship is being self-disciplined along a path of loyalty to someone. Christianity is all about being disciples of Christ.

"Imitate God, therefore, in everything you do, because you are his dear children. Live a life filled with love, following the example of Christ" (Ephesians 5: 1, 2 NLT). Paul admonishes with caution: "Be imitators of me, in so far as I in turn am an imitator of Christ" (1 Corinthians 11: 12 WNT).

Therefore "You must have the same attitude that Christ Jesus had" (Philippians 2: 5 NLT). "Whoever says he abides in him ought to walk in the same way in which he walked" (1 John 2: 6 ESV). Jesus calls us to follow Him (Mark 1: 17).

Being disciples of church leaders is evidence of not being disciples of God.

## Anchor Points

Whenever talents and competencies are properly utilized in church leadership, admiration and respect naturally for these church leaders ooze from the hearts of appreciative church people.

These people more often than not are vulnerable to being led. Therefore, spiritual caution must be taken to point those who are so impressionable away from one's self, to Christ:

*"But God forbid that I should glory,*
*Save in the cross of our Lord Jesus Christ"*
(Galatians 6: 14 KJV).

# SPIRITUAL LESSONS FROM CHURCH POLITICS PERTAINING TO RESOURCES

*"For this is how God loved the world:*
*He gave his unique Son so that everyone who believes*
*in Him might not be lost but have eternal life"*
(John 3: 16 ISV).

What resources are subjects of discrepancy in church organizations? Can church resources really be politicized toward self-benefit?

## Indispensable Resources

*Resources* are means necessary for the existence of an entity and the effecting of precise tasks by that entity. In church organizations some indispensable resources are human resource with a spectrum of knowledge and competencies; assets such as buildings, equipment and machinery etc; and monetary resources.

If the church is what it claims to be, then its task of mission to the world is the greatest work on earth. Consequently, the limited resources that the church has to accomplish its task are sacred and must be wisely and fairly distributed.

The resource of money and its distribution both as remuneration for church workers and means to do church work, seems to be the most problematic in church organizations.

**Survival in the Lord's Work Motif**. Many church workers are so concerned with securing their "bread" in the Lord's work to the extent that they are controlled by church leaders who pay them on behalf of the church organization. Consequently, some church leaders use the threats of dismissal, layoff, reduce in remuneration and benefits, to pressure these workers.

Some workers are so concerned about being able through their employment in the Lord's work, to pay their rent or mortgage, have their health care taken care of, support their families, acquire and maintain a new motor vehicle etc, to the extent that they ignore the organizational inequity in resources distribution. However, they more often than not live their entire work life hoping to have financial stability and security at which time they would then speak out against the resource disparity or other ills of church leadership, because at that time, if they are dismissed, they will survive financially.

Sadly, in most cases, even at retirement, many are still somewhat dependent on their church organizations for the indispensable resource of money. Many of these persons because of the need for money, never become agents of good change acting against wrong in their organization during their entire work life. Paradoxically for many church workers, the need of money is of a higher value than right doing.

**Philosophy of Self-benefit**. Regarding the indispensable resource of money, many church leaders have the philosophy that they, in leading the church in the acquisition of resources, especially monetary resources, must in addition to their remuneration, "set up themselves" and to a lesser degree do the same for some of their close friends, because they say "opportunity comes but once." They are always vigilantly waiting on opportunities to craftily effect this philosophy.

**According to Faith or According to Fault?** The degree of impropriety relative to church resources by many dishonest church leaders varies based on their individual state of irreverence for the things that truly belong to God. Those with faith in God's providence take nothing; those with much conscience take little; and those with little conscience take much.

## Caution

When speaking conclusively about how the resources of church organizations are utilized, whether properly, wasted, or misappropriated, caution must be taken to check the facts, and care must be exercised not to hurt the organization or embarrass individuals.

At the same time commendation for proper utilization of resources and principled actions toward correction where there is wastage and misappropriation, are critical factors, especially pertaining to resources made available for the holy work of God.

## Wasted Resources

In many church organizations financial resources are not properly distributed toward the mission areas of the church. Sometimes exorbitant amounts of money amounting in some cases to millions of dollars are spent, but not on worthwhile programs and projects that positively impact people's lives.

**Impressionists.** Many church leaders in order to make an impression on the people of their territorial domain, waste God's resources on big events, promoting themselves, while from their budget vital areas of church mission receive insignificantly less for their operation.

**Procedural Breach**. Some church leaders misuse the privilege of their power breaching organizational procedures and sometimes policy resulting in the wasting of well needed church resources.

Church resources usually come through great sacrifices of the poor in particular. These resources must be guarded carefully. There is no room for irresponsible and wanton waste of church resources. To whom management of God's resources is given much accountability is required. His resources must not be used for selfish reasons but to glorify Him.

## Diverted Resources

It is a practice for church organizations to have important projects for which appeals for contributions are made. Care must be taken not to divert resources given for a specific church project to another church project without the consent of the donors. If a project is aborted or completed the collecting of donation for that same project must be terminated.

Many church leaders put money collected for specific projects into one pool and freely spend this money with no proper accounting concerning how much money in the pool is commensurate to each project.

An organization, based on assessment of the power invested in boards, committees, and individuals, has the right from its general fund to divert resources it budgeted for one thing to a different area.

Proper diverting of any type of resources must be in the interest of the mission of the organization.

## Resource Distribution Equity

Individual workers, departments, levels of administration within church organizations generally have pointed job descriptions with expected targets to reach within given time slots.

Many church leaders are very forceful and regimental in their expectations of church workers. Good performance of workers causes leaders to have a good report for their superiors. Based on the "ego" in church leaders, they cannot afford it to be otherwise.

**Requisite Amount and Type of Resources**. Problems arise whenever resources to get the job done are not forth coming, and at the same time, the same outcome of the job is demanded. Some leaders are inequitable in their distribution of resources to the extent that some individuals get more than adequate resources to do their jobs while others get below the requisite amount to do the same job.

**Resourcing for Failure**. There are cases in which the distribution of resources by some church leaders, because of church politics, is deliberately designed to let some workers do well and others fail.

Sometimes succeeding leaders do not want to support projects founded by their predecessors. Consequently, these church leaders, in order to cause those projects to die and their founders' names with them, allot to those projects, little or no resources.

## Resource Distribution Disparity

In many church organizations the disparity of amount of resources distributed to departments, levels of administration, classes of workers, and places of work, is blatantly evident.

Academic qualification, the position in organizational hierarchy, discipline and type of work, and tenure of service, are some factors that determine remuneration and benefits to church workers.

Church organizations must ensure that there is a clearly communicated principle-based rationale for disparity of resource distribution, especially when this disparity is within the same category and level of work, and more so pertaining to workers with the same level of qualification and years of service.

Sometimes the position a person holds clearly requires more round the clock work, is more comprehensive, and more stressful as compared with the job of other workers albeit common factors of educational requirement and years of service are the same. There ought not to be any problem with that person getting more.

However, whenever that "more" remuneration and benefits are not merely reflecting a commensurate compensation of the "more" work, rather it reflects an extreme and exorbitant "very much more" remuneration and benefits, then this disparity in the context of Christianity, sets the framework for organizational bickering, bitterness, and politicking for positions.

This framework of extreme disparity is compounded when retirement benefits are similarly attached to leadership positions held during the years of active service in God's work.

## Conclusive Spiritual Lessons

God's ownership of everything is clearly articulated in the Bible. For "the earth is the LORD's, and everything in it" (1 Corinthians. 10: 26 NLT). Humankind is but a caretaker. In our management of God's resources we must always strive for impartiality in remuneration, distribution, and incentives. "Do not pervert justice; do not show partiality to the poor or favoritism to the great" (Leviticus. 19: 15 NIV). To do otherwise is evidence of spiritual impoverishment.

## Anchor Point

Resources for the work must be prudently managed toward properly effecting God's work which includes modeling Christlikeness in the remunerating of church workers.

# SPIRITUAL LESSONS FROM CHURCH POLITICS PERTAINING TO LEGACY

*"Then I looked on all the works that my hands had done and on the labor in which I had toiled; and indeed all was vanity and grasping for the wind. There was no profit under the sun."*

(Ecclesiastes 2:11 NKJV).

What lingers in your mind about church leaders who have retired, died, or moved on to another area of service? What constitute a good legacy of a Christian church leader? How important is leadership legacy?

## Three Essentials

Reflection on the life of Jesus Christ on earth naturally arouses three essentials: How He *came* as a human being; how he *lived* as the Messiah; and how He *left* as the Savior.

The way a church leader comes to office, lives in executing power pertaining to that office, and how the leader leaves from that position, are all critical cumulative sentinels of legacy.

To have good legacies optimized, all these three factors must be positively guarded. Any of these that is adversely negative can minimize or nullify the positive of the other two, and can easily become the permanent legacy by which a leader is remembered way after he of she is gone.

## Contending Legacies

What really is a legacy and how essential is it in the context of church leadership?

A *legacy* is something important or essential that is derived from the past contributions of a person or a people group. More precisely, in the context of a Christian church organization, it is the unique contributions to the work of the Lord that a leader, an administration, or a collective generation of leaders has left behind as assets toward the fulfilling of the mission of Christ.

Many leaders spiritually err by being self-centered, obsessed with their own names and their own legacies to the extent that they fail to pass on the landmark legacies of practice, and doctrines hewed and polished in difficult periods by their predecessors. Hence, paradoxically, their legacy is the destruction of legacy.

Not only do many church leaders erode organizational practices and fail to pass on good traditions, but in order to be new and different, and overly concerned to leave their own names written on edifices, they are unaware that they are demonstrating un-Christian attitudes and methods that are diametrically opposed to the operational principles and policies of their church.

Also, in this selfish quest of their own legacies many church leaders block the wheel of good collective changes and turn their backs on prudent ideas because of where and from whom these ideas emanate. At the same time, quite often good ideas are stolen from others by many church leaders and used as their own. Consequently, personal potential legacies contend for supremacy and the church's structure designed by the founding fathers for proper governance, in many cases is strangled and abused by church leaders in order to spin the wheel of change in the direction of self-centered legacy.

## Legacy Unveiled

In order to pass on good legacies to those who follow, a Christian philosophy of legacy is indispensable. Such philosophy must not merely be an academic exposition but a personal point of reference which guides leadership ascension, performance, and exit.

Simply put, a legacy must be predicated on the premise of continuing God's favor of grace to humanity. It must be principle-based and easily perpetuated by being properly effected and integrated within the church culture. At the same time, it must be of spiritual values in relation to God's ideal for His children.

**People as Legacy**. There are some church leaders who rather than thinking of legacy as values perpetuating the grace of God, see their legacy as people whom they have strategically placed in leadership positions, in order to receive self-benefits even when they have long left the scene of action. Technically these leaders though they have left office physically, through their people-legacy, are still very integrally involved in the leadership of their organization.

Consequently, politics pertaining to people as legacy is very prominent in many Christian church communities. Many church leaders who for one reason or another have to demit an office of leadership position, seek support for whomsoever they considered will most favor their views, guidance, and care after they are gone.

**Compound Legacy**. The politics of legacy becomes more intense whenever some church leaders have cognizance of their personal potential legacies of a program, an institution, a scholarship, a building etc that can bear their names. In these leaders' minds this requires more intense politics because such legacies need people to perpetuate them. Such potential legacies must not die because they are the only entities that bear the names of their founders.

In such circumstances many church leaders get politically involved in an effort to compound their legacy by additionally securing people-legacy to secure their possession and procedural legacies.

**Position as Legacy**. On leaving university, a young pastor notes: "You think I am not going to become President and leave my picture on the wall to inspire my children!" Hence, with this conceptual glitch, many church employees want to literally pass on leadership positions as a legacy or birthright to their children. Others believe that conceptually they must inculcate leadership position in the minds of their children and relative as being a sign of optimal achievement.

Consequently, many church leaders solicit votes for themselves, their relatives, and whomsoever will help them to perpetuate their leadership position-legacy. This leads to nepotism. At times some relatives, who are considered as liabilities to such leadership transgenerational chain, are skipped over.

**Values as Legacy**. Thinking of a late father, what stands out is not how many houses he built, how many cattle he had, or how many acres of land he procured, but his prayer life, morality, and wise counsel. His good legacy lives on.

Remembering one president what stands out are his principle of ethics and his sincerity and other Christian traits. There is a sense of heaven thinking about him. Another president is remembered for his trickery, his comedy, vindictive nature, and disrespect for people.

Those things about them stand out as their most impacting legacies which are validated by people of their times.

## Conclusive Spiritual Lessons

The guide for legacy is found in the word of God. "The grass withers and the flowers fade, but the word of our God stands forever" (Isaiah 40: 8 NLT). Buildings, programs, people, money in financial institutions, and all physical resources are transient and perishable. Virtues last!

True virtues are amplified by Paul the apostle: "Finally, brethren, whatsoever things are true, whatsoever things are honest, whatsoever things are just, whatsoever things are pure, whatsoever things are lovely, whatsoever things are of good report; if there be any virtue, and if there be any praise, think on these thing"(Philippians 4: 8 KJV).

The best legacy is a Christlike character model that guides people despite their rank, position, education, possession, location, and association, to the imperishable kingdom of God.

## Anchor Point

Jesus answered, "My kingdom is not of this world" (St. John 18: 36).

# SPIRITUAL LESSONS FROM CHURCH POLITICS PERTAINING TO FEAR

*"Fear thou not for I am with thee"*
(Isaiah 41: 10 KJV).

Is good church leadership one that requires fear toward getting positive outcomes? How must church workers respond to leaders who use fear tactics toward desired respect and compliance?

## Fear as a Political Tactic

*Fear* is an emotion of anxiety based on the perception of being at a disadvantage in the face of an unfavorable circumstance.

More often than not, church leaders have power to make decisions regarding the lives of employees. They have direct power and influence over committees and boards which generally hire and dismiss workers.

Because church organizations do not normally settle their internal dispute in the secular courts (1

Corinthians 6: 1), and church dispute resolution bodies usually rule in favor of higher level leaders, many church leaders purposely over-stepped policies, circumnavigate laws, and getting away at the disadvantage of workers. Therefore, many church leaders by their craftiness, in one way or another usually have their way in hurting church employees. In this context, many leaders operate with a "Fear me and follow me," or "Do not fear me and feel it" dictum. This is $21^{st}$ century Machiavallianism[1] at its best.

Sure enough the experience of many church workers' "not fearing and feeling it," abounds richly is many present day church organizations: The dismissing of workers; blocking persons in relation to their getting work elsewhere in the organization and sometimes even in other organizations; the cutting of remuneration; the reassigning to harder tasks but with the same or less pay; the transferring to more difficult terrains etc. Consequently, many church workers fear their church leaders.

### Fearful Countenances

Many church leaders are "perfectly pleasant and jovial" when relating as public relations agents for their organizations, but when they relate to their workers, they do so with stern countenances.

Stern countenances are often associated with firmness pertaining to church leadership. Many church leaders' way of governance is to use stern facial expressions to communicate to workers, especially those with whom they have no close acquaintance of friendship.

In meetings to decide disciplinary measures to be meted out to workers who in one way or another violate organizational code of ethics, stern countenances of church leaders are sometime intentionally designed to drive fear into the hearts of the violators.

**Fearful Words and Gestures**

Many church leaders in addition to stern facial expressions, use threats, and make insinuations regarding possible unfavorable outcomes pertaining to workers' livelihood.

The tone of voice with which threatening words are spoken and gestures of body are also use to drive fear into workers toward compliance. Sometimes this compliance has to do with political support of a church leader in relation to gaining or retaining leadership power.

The tone allows words to stick to memory. At church election sessions to choose top leaders, there are at times threats in stern tones from incumbent church leaders to rival leaders such as "If you run against me, make sure you do not lose, because if you lose, I am going to send you to the most challenging area to work." This is to intimidate rival leaders toward withdrawing candidacy for the positions.

Sometimes the rival leaders win and do to the then incumbents the thing they threatened to others. Consequently, the odyssey of fear in these church organizations is perpetuated as a vicious cycle.

## Fearful Acts

Whenever workers in general see church leaders act outside of Christian virtues in dismissing, cutting benefits, blocking employment, demoting fellow employees, and getting away with it, it naturally drives fear into their own hearts, because they themselves could be next.

Moreover when church leaders of stern countenances speak fearful words of threats and go on to carry out those threats, those leaders have developed a reputation of being feared.

Acts validate intention and way of life. Many church leaders rejoice on the fact that they are feared by others. It becomes their permanent modus operandi.

## Conflict Creators

Conflict is the daily bread provided by hard but repulsive work of many church leaders. Whenever there is no conflict these leaders are uneasy. They thrive on conflict. They are nourished by it. They hunger for its substance.

These church leaders seem to look for creative ways to stir up a conflict especially with those who seem not to be their disciples. This they do in order to test and find seemingly tenable reasons get rid of some workers. This often results in many church workers having a fearful uneasiness because of these deliberate conflict creators.

## Conclusive Spiritual Lessons

The Bible declares that those who delight in peace-making are blessed and are the sons of God (Matthew 5: 9). Implicitly, those who stir up conflict are not "blessed" neither are they called the sons of God.

At the same time "Love has no fear, because perfect love expels all fear. If we are afraid, it is for fear of punishment, and this shows that we have not fully experienced his perfect love" (1 John 1: 18 NLT).

In all fearful situations God is with His children. He reminds us: "Fear thou not; for I am with thee: be not dismayed; for I am thy God: I will strengthen thee; yea, I will help thee; yea, I will uphold thee with the right hand of my righteousness" (Isaiah 41: 10 KJV). "But even if you suffer for doing what is right, God will reward you for it. So don't worry or be afraid of their threats" (1 Peter 3: 14 NLT).

## Anchor Point

"Let us think of ways to motivate one another to acts of love and good works" (Hebrews 10: 34 NLT).

# SPIRITUAL LESSONS FROM CHURCH POLITICS PERTAINING TO HUMOR

*"I also will laugh at your calamity;*
*I will mock when your fear comes"*
(Proverbs 1: 26 KJV).

I s there a time and place for humor in church leadership? Can jokes be serious business in church governance? Can jokes be spiritually and professionally detrimental to workers in God's cause?

## Happiness

*Happiness* is a pleasurable or joyful state of mind. It results from being satisfied based on the realization of something which is perceived as good. Christians are generally of a happy disposition notwithstanding transient bouts of mitigating circumstances.

True happiness is a natural result of being connected to Christ. Happiness for the Christian is a lifestyle. For Christians, sad occasions and incidents do not counter the general state of happiness, they affirm it because of the consciousness that all causes for sadness will eventually be banished by Christ.

**Value-based Humors**. Humor within church organizations generally erupts the spirit of happiness into laughter bringing the relief of stress and enhancing production. Humor for Christians must not conflict with Christian values. If it does, then it is not to be found humorous in the eyes of Christians. Values must be essential ingredients of humors in all church organizations.

Church leaders must make every effort to create work environs that foster happiness for all workers.

## Crafty Humors

In today's society the term comedy implies a well organized intentionally arranged context of humor spoken and acted to the proportion of being commercialized. Comedy is for professionals in the business of humor.

Many church leaders though, are as skillful with humor as professional comedians are, but only that the dividends of church leader comedians are not instant monetary assets, but in many cases are emotionally hurt and confused people, especially the spiritually young. In many circumstances laughter is present but true happiness is absent, and jokes are but the psychological facade of deep sadness in the hearts of these leader comedians.

**Humor and Callousness**

Many church leaders whether they are talking to one individual, chairing meetings, or addressing a large body of people, are excellent at using humor to get and hold people's attention.

**Humor Referring to Workers**. While many church leaders are respectable, pure, and sincere in their use of humor to clarify issues, encourage, and affirm workers, some church leaders are not.

There are some church leaders who use humor to disrespect workers directly and indirectly; as fun regarding the downfall of others; as joy of being victorious over others pertaining to being elected to a leadership position; as means to belittle others; and as sarcasm regarding the success of others.

The intent and content of jokes used by church leaders toward making others laugh, speak volumes of the righteousness or callousness of those leaders.

**Humor as a Means to an End.** Many church leaders misuse humor. They use humor to get the attention and win the hearts of members, and while the members are distracted in laughter, these leader-comedians suddenly change to a tone of sternness and overtly or subtly disrespect the members or workers, sometimes to the extent of taking away their constitutional right to speak, not allowing them to make suggestions or ask questions. These members usually get very aggravated but find it difficult to show because they were just laughing. Funny, is not it?

In the state of the members' elation, the church leaders have their ways toward critical decisions. Their humor used in this context is but a means to an end. In some cases, the leaders end their discourse again giving jokes and the same disrespected aggravated members laugh. The leaders walk away and also laugh, but not at their own jokes, but at the members naivety.

## Conclusive Spiritual Lessons

In many contexts of church organizations, laughing together can be a very sad thing when in reality bitterness against each other truly saturates the hearts; and being genuinely sad together because people are hurting, is a profound reason for happiness because of this bonding love.

The Bible speaks against those "who rejoice to do evil, and delight in the perverseness of the wicked" (Proverbs 2: 14 KJV). "Love does not delight in evil but rejoices with the truth" (1 Corinthians 13: 5 NIV). Rejoicing in the sense of being entertained by evil making mockery of right doing is spiritual insanity.

When Belshazzar king of Babylon in his merriment desecrated the holy vessels of the Lord, God wrote with unseen hands "thou art weighed in the balances, and art found wanting" (See Dan 5). That very night serious judgment of being overthrown was meted out to the king. Some church leaders fall at the peak of their sacrilegious comedy.

"Be sober-minded; be watchful. Your adversary the devil prowls around like a roaring lion, seeking someone to devour" (1 Peter 5: 8 ESV).

## Anchor Point

"Rejoice in the Lord always: and again I say, Rejoice" (Philippians 4: 4 KJV). Christian humor pertaining to God's work must be of sound moral values and ethical principles.

# SPIRITUAL LESSON FROM CHURCH POLITICS PERTAINING TO GRIEF

*"Jesus wept."*
(St John 11: 35 KJV)

*"A time to cry . . . . A time to grieve"*
(Ecclesiastes 3: 4 NLT).

How must church leaders relate to their own grief or that of another? Can grief be misused toward political intent? Is the cause of grief associated with personal faults?

## The Inevitability of Grief

*Grief* is an intense emotion of pain resulting from a great loss, especially the loss of the life of a loved one. Grief is inevitable in a sinful world and eventually in one way or another will impact and affect each person. No church leader, worker, or member is exempt.

The price for grief has been paid for by the blood of Jesus. Whatever or whomsoever is the loss, grief will be truly endured only within the "Blessed Hope"-the resurrection to eternal life at the second coming of Jesus.

## Tough-Guy Syndrome

Many church leaders believe that to express their pain caused by the loss of their loved ones, is to appear weak before their colleagues and members. They believe they must always appear to be the tough guys. Hence, their humanity is suppressed by their leadership position and pride.

To be a church leader means to be a reputable sample of the body of people whom you lead. Jesus himself wept and was "acquainted with grief" (St John 11: 35; and Isaiah 53: 3). The imagery of great Bible leaders mourning speaks profoundly of the humanity of earth's greatest leaders and the humbling impact which grief wrought upon their hearts (Genesis 23: 2; 1 Kings 14: 13; 1Samuels 16: 1; and Job 1: 20).

Leaders seem more real and genuine in relating to their grief as ordinary humans do, but appear false and cold when because they are church leaders they act as super-humans.

**Personal Experience**: One leader when asked why he treated his workers so harshly and disrespectfully, reported that a loved one of his had died and his contained and postponed grieving resulted in his crude behaviors to his workers, even those who were his close friends. This seems like *displacement*—a form of psychological defense mechanism in which a person directs the emotion of anxiety to a substitute target.[1]

Unexpressed grief can lead to social, spiritual, physical, and mental problems.

**Bad Theology**. Many church leaders who are victims of the tough guy syndrome embrace the view that "heaven is real therefore do not grieve about losses on earth." The Bible says: "Brothers, we do not want you to . . . grieve like the rest of men, who have no hope" (1 Thessalonians 4: 13 NLT). The contextual clause is "like the rest of men, who have no hope." We are to grieve or sorrow but as those who have hope. We can grieve that the realization of the hope is not "now" as in this very moment; therefore, until then there remains the void of our loved ones.

Leaders too must empty their souls with grief at their loss. It is understood that some leaders especially males are better at expressing their grief privately. If so, their speaking about it publicly will help to inform those whom they lead, that their leaders are fully human.

## Mirages

Whenever there is a loss, support is needed. Such support varies from presence, prayer, power, and sometimes present. Many church leaders who suffer great loss are sometimes suspicious as to how genuine is such support. They silently withdraw within the grieving chambers of their minds and ask many questions. It is one thing when people support you because you are their leader. That is expected, and abundantly so. But it is another thing when such support is based only on expected favors and friendship that mitigate against future equitable treatment to other employees.

**Motive.** The thanksgiving funeral service of leaders' loved ones whether father, mother, husband, wife, children etc, usually in church circles attracts large crowds and a wide spectrum of other leaders of the same ilk as well as leaders of different types.

In such circumstances, some church leaders literally beg to personally get an opportunity (even to the extent of taking someone else off the program) to participate in speech. Sometimes this is with ulterior motives, not necessarily to genuinely bring commiseration, but mainly to make an impression, to show and magnify one's self for political reasons. This case is really exceptional, because generally church leaders and workers are genuine in their expression of grief.

**Extremes**. Many people because of their ulterior motives go to the extreme to support leaders in their losses to the extent that they literally crowd out others thereby hindering a wider variety of support.

## Attributing Causes

Worse than the foregoing is the attributing of causes why leaders suffer losses. Surprisingly, in many church organizations, whenever a leader suffers many persons attribute the leader's loss to the leader's wickedness, claiming that God is giving the leader a "wake-up" and "watch your way" warning.

While circumstance of loss more often than not, naturally causes well thinking spiritual persons to check their lives for spiritual shortcomings, it is never in the domain of any human being to attribute moral causes to a person's losses.

## Protracted Grief Mode

Many church leaders who are very supportive of other church workers during their time of grief, gained their respect during that time if never before.

**Keeping Persons in a Grief Mode**. Consequently, some of these church leaders try to keep persons in the grief mode by constantly mentioning in one way or another, the loss, more or less to keep such person's respect because the leaders' support is associated with the loss. This is a sort of slavery through grief.

**Keeping One's Self in a Grief Mode.** A political tactic of some church leaders who have had tragedy and great losses, is that of publicly reminding members who have the power to vote them into church office about these tragedies. Therefore, years after their loss, they preach about it, pray aloud about it, introduce themselves with it as if it happened today and they are hurting. This they do to psychologically indirectly seek sympathy for political support.

## Conclusive Spiritual Lessons

It is appointed to all men to die (Hebrews 9: 27) because the wages of sin is death (Romans 6: 23) and all have sinned (Romans 3: 23). Consequently, each person's bereavement must be treated as our own bereavement as one human race. In such case, "The heart of the wise is in the house of mourning, but the heart of fools is in the house of pleasure" (Ecclesiastes 7: 4 NIV). Our mourning with those who are bereaved must be spiritual and sincere.

God promises : "I will turn their mourning into joy, and will comfort them, and make them rejoice from their sorrow" (Jeremiah 31: 13 KJV). Whatever we do on behalf of persons in bereavement ought to be, to genuinely comfort their bereavement and to supportively transform their sorrow over time into joy. It is all about them, never about us.

## Anchor Point

To His wayward children "even now, declares the Lord, return to me with all your heart, with fasting and weeping and mourning" (Joel 2: 12 NIV). This is very applicable to whomsoever misuses grief toward self benefit.

# SPIRITUAL LESSONS FROM CHURCH POLITICS PERTAINING TO EDUCATION

*"Study to shew thyself approved unto God"*
(2 Timothy 2: 15 KJV).

D oes education always enhance church work? Can education be wasted in church organization? Is the access and quest for more education factors of problems in 21st century churches?

## Education as a Necessity

*Education* in the context of church work, is the formal or informal acquisition of knowledge and wisdom to relevantly utilize this knowledge to effect church mission.

The spectrum of educational disciplines relevant to church mission directly or indirectly, is very wide. Whether it is theology, health science, computer programming, philosophy, cosmetology, mechanics, linguistics, astronomy, culinary arts and the list is endless; there is a place for all this knowledge in 21st century church organizations. God is the source and center of all knowledge.

Not only is the spectrum wide but the levels of offerings as never before range from certification to termination. Terminal degrees of Ph. D, Th. D, D. Min, Psy. D and others are many more than they have every been in history. The dam of education has broken and church workers are diving in.

## Motives

Academic degrees do not only mean the fulfillment of a prescribed course of knowledge and competencies in a particular discipline, but in many cases this acquisition means more remuneration, and promotion in rank and status.

Some people get more education just to prove a point that they have the capacity so to do. Therefore, they get a doctoral degree mainly to be called Doctor. They believe that it means "respect."

On the other hand, many church workers pursue education in order to discover knowledge that is useful to enhance their mission making better contributions to the growth of their organizations.

At the same time, many other church leaders become judgmental and suspicious of many workers who have an apparent insatiable thirst for knowledge. These leaders are quick to conclude regarding the motives of those who pursue education. One must not judge the motives of others.

## Keeping Education Limited

In church organizations there are limitations to educational pursuit. Some of these limitations are justifiable based on budgetary and other reasons and some are political.

**Limited to Certification**. Many church organizations require continuing education for their workers, but that is only at the level of certification which the organization takes care of financially, never at the degree level.

**Limited to Levels of Academic Diplomas**. Some organizations part-sponsor their workers' education up to the Masters level but not beyond. After that level workers who want to do a doctoral degree have to fully finance it from their personal finances.

**Limited to Quota**. In many cases, some organizations have a time table and quota of workers who can be sponsored at any one time.

**Limited to Disciplines**. Some church organizations will not sponsor their workers to pursue studies in particular disciplines.

**Limited to Institutions**. At the same time, some organizations will not sponsor their workers to pursue studies at institutions other than their own church institutions.

**Limited to Friends and Relatives**. Church politics become obvious in cases in which many church leaders are slow to approve organizational sponsorship to workers who are not considered their supporters, but at the same time are quick to approve sponsorship for their friends and relatives.

These church leaders wrongly use their authority to make this asset of educational opportunity firstly available to their relatives and friends. In some cases while mainly choosing their relatives and supporters, in order for their partiality not to be very blatant, some leaders also chose a "token," another person who is not considered their friend or supporter.

## Education as Liability

Many church leaders see the education of some workers as a liability. This is partly because in their eyes these persons are more exposed, more critical and creative in their thinking, more knowledgeable not only of what to be done in the context of church leadership but now have new and creative ways to get the job done.

The "more" educated persons from the perspective of some church leaders are now threats to leadership positions. These church leaders do something about that perception or reality. They act to greatly minimize the "perceived" threat of being replaced by these "more" educated persons.

Because of the perceived threats these workers are sometimes transferred and reassigned so-called "important" duties, their academic achievements kept as secret, sidelined and silenced, and negatives about them are construed, concocted, and conveyed.

They become liability in two ways: conceptual and actual. Conceptual in the sense of being a liability to the leaders' positions. Actual in the sense of being reassigned to new jobs sometimes outside of their specialty, hence, they have to start from scratch and thereby their contributions to the organization is lower than it was prior to their "education."

**Education as an Asset**

Education empowers and in the proper operational context is definitely an asset.

Many church organizations seek to empower their work by making favorable policy and budgetary allotments toward their workers' education. They also rejoice over their workers' educational achievements and place and promote them to where they can be most effective in advancing the church's mission. Great!

Many church organizations conduct ongoing seminars and workshops to keep their workers competent and current. This enhances the input and outcome of their work.

Education is an asset in the proper operational context, both to the educated person and the workplace.

## Education Manipulated

Education can be wrongly manipulated in church organizations.

**Philosophy.** There was a time in the way distant past when people were classified as being in the categories of head, heart, or senses.[1] Heads were philosophers and were considered to be most eligible to become leaders because more or less, it was thought that they were closer to God-the absolute mind; hearts were those thought to be less intelligent, but they had passion and bravery and were therefore chosen as soldiers; while the common people had a dominant crave to satisfy the senses (appetites). The latter were classified as being least intelligent.

Many church persons seem to demand church leadership position as "rulers" solely because of their education. Quite often they manipulate others who are considered less educated.

**Plagiarism.** In our age many church leaders hold the views that the best brains are of necessity the top church leaders. In many cases it is the utilized ideas of the people below top leaders that keep the organization current, relevant, and viable.

However, many leaders use the educational perspectives of other workers to build up the organization and themselves without even recognizing the sources from which organizational building perspectives were derived.

It becomes even worse when church leaders claim ideas and perspectives of other workers as their own. It is at its worst when written works documented by workers are totally claimed by church leader as theirs.

**Requirements**. In regards to the filling of available work positions, many church leaders change the requirements up or down to wrongly favor whomsoever they wish to get the job. This approach at times is to the detriment of the organization. Educational requirements are generally set with required outcomes in mind, and at times these are not forthcoming because people who are not qualified for these tasks are assigned to these positions based on favoritism.

## Educational Abuse.

Whenever church leaders are placed in church positions of which they have little or no educational competence. They in turn delegate the work to others who are specifically educated for these tasks. These church leaders just bear the name while others do the tasks making these church leaders look far above their real competence.

In many cases, whenever the organization searches for someone to fill those same leadership positions, conveniently the out-going church leaders seemingly have a sudden lapse of memory and refuse to identify anyone around with the competencies to do the job. Using another person's education to advance one's self without any interest in that person's advancement is educational abuse.

Also, many leaders in church organizations use the idea that they are more educated in relation to their academic degrees, to boss around, talk down to, and humiliate others who supposedly lack knowledge. In so doing they give the impression that education makes some people more important than others, therefore, those less educated are inferior. To use education toward this end is a form of educational abuse.

## Two Paradoxes

Regarding perusing higher education, many church leaders complain that church workers in their organizations are too taken up with such goal. They complain that this negatively affects the mission of the Lord. Maybe it can if not properly planned. However, the paradox is that some of these same leaders firstly ensure that their friends and family members in the organization and themselves, get on an academic program at the highest level.

The second paradox is that after many church leaders achieve terminal academic degrees, they now strongly admonish workers not to focus on studying but on Christ because He is soon to come. Are studying for an academic degree and living for Christ mutually exclusive?

## Conclusive Spiritual Lessons

Whether competence comes through natural or spiritual giftedness, it must be use for the edification of the church thereby effecting the message of the gospel in the lives of people.

True knowledge must be sought: "Fear of the LORD is the foundation of true knowledge, but fools despise wisdom and discipline" (Proverbs 1: 7 NLT). Church leaders must firstly truly educate themselves in fearing God, and secondly treat others as they themselves would want to be treated and without prejudice open up the avenues of education to all workers recognizing and utilizing those workers to build up the work of God. To each of these persons the Lord will say: "Well done, you good and faithful servant" (Matthew 25: 21 NKJV).

"Do nothing out of selfish ambition or vain conceit, but in humility consider others better than yourselves" (Philippians 2: 3 NIV).

## Anchor Point

"The man who thinks he knows something does not yet know as he ought to know" (1 Corinthians 8: 2 NIV).

# SPIRITUAL LESSONS FROM CHURCH POLITICS PERTAINING TO UNDOING, REDOING, AND OUTDOING

*"I have planted, Apollos watered; but*
*God gave the increase"*
(1 Corinthians 3: 6 KJV).

How ought church leaders to relate to the success of their predecessors? Is there a place in God's work for competitive contributions? Is the spirit of undoing, redoing, and outdoing appropriate in church governance?

## Undoing

In pursuit of minimizing or eliminating the legacies of preceding church administrations, many church leaders undo great innovations. Consequently, good projects are stopped, committed workers are laid off, funds are diverted, policies are changed, and supports in one way or another withdrawn.

More often than not, whenever great innovations are undone by self-centered church leaders, people suffer, hope diminishes, resources lost, and time and effort wasted.

## Redoing

In other circumstances, many church leaders although they do not undo great contributions to God's church by previous administrations, they re-launch these same ideas and innovations, but in their own names claiming them toward honors for themselves on a church, community, regional, or even sometimes on national level.

Knowing how to "play their cards," subsequently they get their honors without themselves being honorable. They rejoice externally but internally they have streaks and shades of unhappiness in their hearts. The latter depends whether or not the Holy Spirit is allowed to bring them inner conviction.

At the same time, many good church leaders properly assess projects and programs innovated by their predecessors and wisely re-launch them to make them more known, better and more supported but not without recognition and respect for those from whom those ideas originally sprung.

## Outdoing

The attitude and efforts of some church leaders to outdo those leaders who have gone before, spring from a self-concept of being inferior, therefore they are self-driven to prove their ability.

The ego and spiritual immaturity of a leader are at their highest levels whenever his or her speech is proliferated with rhetoric of "I am the first."

Furthermore, imagine how ludicrous it is for a church leader to say that he or she is the first to pay so much salary to workers, first to be the leader of so many members, first to travel to so many places, first to be so educated, when naturally the trajectory of any growing organization over time would see these growths.

Even in cases where a church leader has led very well in growing the organization, true godliness and humility ensure that one does not beat one's chest in self praise. Bragging about being a better deacon or director, a better president or chief executive officer than others who have gone on ahead, is reflective of a deficient character. Many church leaders fail to understand that they ought to be representatives of Christ's humility.

While many church leaders boast of being the first in good things, ironically members usually mutter that they the said leaders are the first and worst in some bad things.

### Conclusive Spiritual Lessons

"But you must not brag about being grafted in to replace the branches that were broken off. You are just a branch, not the root" (Romans 11: 18 NLT). The apostle Paul noted: "I have planted, Apollos watered; but God gave the increase" (1 Corinthians 3: 6 KJV).

## Anchor Point

God is able to "make you perfect in every good work to do his will, working in you that which is well pleasing in his sight, through Jesus Christ; to whom be glory for ever and ever. Amen" (Hebrews 13: 20, 21 KJV).

# CONSCIENCE AND
# CONCLUSIONS

*"Let us hear the conclusion of the whole matter:*
*Fear God, and keep his commandments:*
*for this is the whole duty of man"*
(Proverbs 12: 13 KJV).

What is a spiritually formed conscience? How is conscience relevant to one's conclusive exit from church employment or from a church leadership position?

## Spiritually Formed Conscience

*Conscience* from a Christian perspective is a personal, mental, and moral index that concludes whether or not a thought or an act is right or wrong. Otherwise put, our perceptive awareness that emanates from our moral data bank, from which we make conclusions regarding right and wrong. It is the psychological faculty which differentiates between good and bad.

The Bible speaks about many persons in the latter times "having their own conscience seared with a hot iron" (I Timothy. 4: 2 NKJV). The conscience described as being seared with a hot iron, refers to a person's state of mind which leads to attitudes and behaviors contrary to Christian virtues.

**Indulgence and Conscience**. Indulgence either strengthens or weakens conscience. "Woe unto them that call evil good, and good evil; that put darkness for light, and light for darkness; that put bitter for sweet, and sweet for bitter!" (Isaiah. 5: 20 KJV). A spiritually formed conscience is one that is based on biblical values reinforced in the lives of Christians by God's Spirit over time.

The essence of conscience is that, we in some ways cannot escape ourselves, particularly in our declining, concluding, post church leadership or retirement years.

In these years, Christian people normally scrutinize themselves in relation to their execution of duty along the spectrum of their career, whether in church leadership or any other discipline of life. There, it is too late to make changes to our past attitudes, decisions, and actions.

## Exit and Conclusions

Many church leaders as they increase in years and decline in strength, come to the realization that they are not invincible. Based on organizational policies, they have to give up power. They have to go. They have to retire.

**Critical Thoughts**. For a while they focus on their tangibles spanning their families, their real estate, their securities, but know that these things have nothing to do with their eternal destiny. Critical questions of "Have I been who the Lord called me to be?" and "Have I done what He wanted me to do?" dominate their thoughts.

However, without a conscience that is spiritually formed, our conclusions of ourselves regarding our attitudes, decisions, and actions regarding people, and execution of duties, are prone to serious inaccuracies.

**Leadership Model**. Some church leaders develop a top-down leadership model that is not congruent to the servant-leadership model of Jesus. However, many of these leaders at their exit from denominational work wrongly conclude that they had modeled Christlike servant-leadership. A wrong conclusion reflects a messy value system which lacks the influence of the Holy Spirit

**Misuse of Power.** Also, some leaders who have misused and abused their power strangely seem to have no clue regarding the proper use of power within the context of the Christian life. They conclude that they have been great spiritual leaders.

**Inaccurate Conclusions**. Whenever church leaders have left their leadership positions by retirement or reassignment and in their mind are not able to differentiate between right and wrong, and between asset and liability, it results in seriously inaccurate conclusions regarding self-assessment. Consequently, many of these leaders pamper and praise themselves as great achievers, while at the same time those, whom they have served, justifiably praise God for relieving them of these tyrannical and ungodly leaders who are now out of their lives and that the church can now move to its mission of godliness.

**Sadness and Regrets.** On the other hand, many church leaders spend their declining retirement years in deep sadness and regrets pertaining to how in the execution of their duties they treated God, His work and His people. Hopefully, regret lead to repentance and confession.

## Conclusive Spiritual Lessons

"God shall bring every work into judgment" (Ecclesiastes 12: 14: KJV). "And, behold, I come quickly; and my reward is with me, to give every man according as his work shall be" (Revelation 22: 12 KJV).

God's reward to the righteous generally is applicable to each church leader who has been a great servant: "His lord said unto him, well done, thou good and faithful servant: thou hast been faithful over a few things, I will make thee ruler over many things: enter thou into the joy of thy lord" (Matthew 25: 21 KJV).

On the other hand, each leader who misrepresents Christ without repentance will receive the consequence as each wicked person: "Cast ye the unprofitable servant into outer darkness: there shall be weeping and gnashing of teeth" (Matthew 25: 30 KJV).

## Anchor Point

"Be not deceived; God is not mocked: for whatsoever a man soweth, that shall he also reap" (Galatians 6: 7 KJV). "Sow to yourselves in righteousness, reap in mercy" (Hosea 10: 12 KJV).

# NOTES

## Chapter 1

[1]J. Coleman (2000*). A history of political thought: From ancient Greece to early Christianity.* Malden, MA: Blackwell (p.21).

[2]H. Dalen & L. Ziegler (1977, p. 1). *Introduction to political science: People, politics and perception.* Englewood Cliffs, N J: Prentice-Hall.

## Chapter 2

[1]F. Flaniken (2006). Is the Bible relevant to servant leadership? *The Journal of Applied Christian Leadership. 1*, 32-39.

[2]H. Finzel (2000). *The top ten mistakes leaders make.* Colorado Springs, CO: Cook Communications Ministries.

[3]W. D. Longstaff, Take Time To Be Holy, *In Seventh-day Adventist Church Hymnal.* Hagerstown, MD: Review and Herald Publishing Association.

[4]D. H. Stevenson (1999). Spiritual maturity Index. In P. Hill & R. Hood (Eds.), *Measures of religiosity*. Birmingham, AL: Religious Education Press.

[5]Ibid.

## Chapter 3
[1]Napoleon Hill (1937). *Think and Grow Rich*. Chicago, Illinois: Combined Registry Company. p. 14.

## Chapter 5
[1]D. Johnson & J. Van Vonderen (1991). *The subtle power of spiritual abuse*. Minneapolis, MN: Bethany House.

[2]D. S. Whitney (2002). *Ten questions to diagnose your spiritual faith*. Colorado Springs CO: Navpress.

## Chapter 8
[1]E. G. White (1898). *The desire of ages*. Mountain View, CA: Pacific Press.

## Chapter 10
[1]G. Orwell (1946). *Animal Farm*. London: Penguin Group.

## Chapter 15
[1]Mechiavallianism: "the political theory . . . of the view that politics is amoral and that any means however

unscrupulous can justifiably be used in achieving political power." (Http://www.merriam-webster.com/dictionary/Machiavellian)

## Chapter 17
[1]D. Sue, D. Sue, & S. Sue (2003), *Understanding Abnormal Behavior.* New York: Boston. Haughton Milflin Company (47).

## Chapter 18
[1]J. Matthews (2001). *Philosophical foundations of education and psychology.* Andrews University, Berrien Springs, Michigan.

# INDEX TO SUBJECTS